Gallery Books

Editor Peter Fallon

PIRANDELLOS

Thomas Kilroy

PIRANDELLOS

Two plays

SIX CHARACTERS IN SEARCH OF AN AUTHOR

and

HENRY (*after* HENRY IV)

Gallery Books

Pirandellos
is first published
simultaneously in paperback
and in a clothbound edition
on 14 December 2007.

The Gallery Press
Loughcrew
Oldcastle
County Meath
Ireland

© Thomas Kilroy 2007

ISBN 97
97

A CIP catalogue record for this book
is available from the British Library.

Thomas Kilroy has asserted his right to
be identified as the author of this Work.

Contents

SIX CHARACTERS IN SEARCH
OF AN AUTHOR

Characters

The Acting Company
FIRST ACTOR
FIRST ACTRESS
SECOND ACTOR
SECOND ACTRESS
DIRECTOR
ASM, *a woman*

The Family
FATHER
MOTHER
SON
STEPDAUGHTER
TWO CHILDREN, A BOY AND A GIRL

MADAME PACE, *a woman who appears and disappears*

This version of *Six Characters in Search of an Author* was first performed at the Abbey Theatre, Dublin, on 1 May 1996, with the following cast:

SECOND ACTOR	David Wilmot
FIRST ACTRESS	Susan Fitzgerald
SECOND ACTRESS	Mary O'Driscoll
FIRST ACTOR	Brian McGrath
DIRECTOR	Owen Roe
ASM	Fionnuala Murphy
FATHER	Gerard McSorley
STEPDAUGHTER	Alison McKenna
MOTHER	Barbara Brennan
CHILDREN	Rory Kennan/Katie Monnelly Donal Ryan/Jessica Barnes
MADAME PACE	Olwen Fouere
Direction	John Crowley
Design	Tom Piper
Lighting	Nick McCall

ACT ONE

Sound: Walking feet on a hard surface. A large projection screen as front drop. Moving/slide images of the Family, walking: FATHER; MOTHER *with the two children,* BOY *and* GIRL, *close beside her, holding hands;* SON *and* STEPDAUGHTER. *They are walking along an empty, bleak road (artificial, stylized stage setting?), their backs to camera and to us. We are following them.*

Pirandello's suggested ages for Family:

FATHER *'about fifty'*
LITTLE GIRL *'four years'*
LITTLE BOY *'little more than ten'*
SON *'about twenty'*
(MOTHER *and* STEPDAUGHTER *not given)*

They are dressed in 'Sunday best', vintage nineteen forties or fifties: clearly a family of some means. FATHER *in solid tweeds, crombie coat,* MOTHER *in widow's black, hat and veil down over her face.* STEPDAUGHTER *in black/greys. They, and the* LITTLE BOY *and* LITTLE GIRL, *wear black mourning diamond patches on their arms. The* STEPDAUGHTER *is to one side in the group and the* SON *lags behind. Hold this image for a few minutes to establish a grim journeying to Nowhere. Then fade and fly out the screen.*

Behind this: Upstage, a raised thrust stage out from the back wall. The back wall is another, identical projection screen, now white, unlit. Downstage, lower level, a rehearsal space, chairs, a table, scripts, coffee cups etc.

ACTOR 2 *(youngish),* ACTRESS 1 *(older) and* ACTRESS 2 *(same as* ACTOR 2*) stroll on for rehearsal.*

ACTOR 2 But why Pirandello?
ACTRESS 2 You mean why do a Pirandello play?
ACTOR 2 Yeah.
ACTRESS 1 He's a modern classic, dear. Tradition — You have heard of tradition?

ACTOR 2 Tradition! Give me a break!

ACTRESS 2 Oh, what's the fuss? You do what's in front of you. You do it as well as you can. That's theatre.

ACTOR 2 Oh no it's not theatre! That's just the point. Nowadays theatre has to prove its right to exist. Why are we here? Eh? Now? In this place? Because we believe, that's why! We believe that theatre can prove itself! Right?

ACTRESS 1 My dear. Listen to me. Theatre doesn't have to prove anything. Never has. Never will.

ACTOR 2 Wrong again, I'm afraid! The days when theatre could take things for granted are long gone. (*Ironical*) Alas, alack. The days of elitist, smug, class-ridden, sexist —

ACTRESS 1 Oh, dear God —

ACTOR 2 — self-satisfied theatre are long gone. Like everything else, nowadays, theatre has to earn its right to speak —

ACTRESS 2 Do you mean sell tickets?

ACTOR 2 I mean *reach* people where they really are! In their real lives, that's what I mean —

ACTRESS 1 I hate it when people use that word 'real' in the theatre. It always leads to dreadful costumes. Anyway, Pirandello reaches real people —

ACTOR 2 How?

ACTRESS 1 In what he writes about — the human imagination!

ACTRESS 2 And power. The way he writes about power —

ACTRESS 1 — the strange, bizarre ways the imagination works —

ACTRESS 2 — and family life, yes, indeed, don't forget family life —

ACTOR 2 Not in what we're working on here, he doesn't. It's not even half there —

ACTRESS 2 But that's the whole point of it! It's meant to be only half there. It's mean to be incomplete. Just like everyday life, as a matter of fact —

ACTRESS 1 I'll take half finished Pirandello any day to — Though, mind you, I have to say, I do have some problems with the text —

ACTOR 1 *arrives, a little breathlessly. Older generation.*

ACTOR 2 Bet *he* doesn't have any problems with the text —

ACTOR 1 What, what? Director's not here, is he? Not late, am I? Dreadful traffic — if there's one thing I can't stand it's being late for rehearsal. It's simply not on, as far as I'm concerned.

ACTRESS 1 (*To* ACTOR 1) Pay no attention to him, come and sit down.

ACTOR 1 Sounding off again, is he?

ACTOR 2 Last thing I'll say is that we're going to have to discover more than we have so far in this (*script*), if we're to go on —

ACTOR 1 Couldn't agree with you more, there. Do you think I should bring that up?

ACTRESS 2 Maybe we will discover something more? That's what we're here for, isn't — ?

DIRECTOR *and* ASM *enter, he in his early thirties, she somewhat older.*

DIRECTOR Did I hear the sound of discord? Great, great! Just what we need to get us moving! Morning all, mind if we start right in? Without the usual confab? That OK with everyone? Got to move a bit faster today, I'm afraid. Pick up the problems as we go along.

ACTOR 2 We were talking about Pirandello. Whether it's even worthwhile doing him in this day and age.

DIRECTOR Heard that. Let's just see whether it is or not?

ACTOR 2 Fine with me. Only questioning, that's all.

ASM From the top, is it?

DIRECTOR From the top it is. Right? Thank you —

ASM The prostitute scene, everybody. (*Announce-*

ment) 'Father and Stepdaughter on. Mother and Son stand by for the moment.'

> ACTOR 1 *and* ACTRESS 1 *take seats by the table.* ACTOR 2 *and* ACTRESS 2 *stand to one side, all looking at scripts.*

ACTOR 1 I'm sorry about this and after your, well, what you've just said and all, but do you mind if I say something before we start? I feel as if I don't know these people somehow. I mean, take the Father here. On the one hand, he seems a decent old — I mean, he does suffer himself, doesn't he? Suffers a lot, I'd say. On the other hand, he seems to put everyone around him through absolute hell, his Stepdaughter here, (*Toward other* ACTORS) his wife, their Son, abuse, incest, you name it —

ACTOR 2 Same problem here.

ACTOR 1 I don't *know* these people. Know what I mean?

DIRECTOR That's just the point! We don't *have* to know them in that way! There's just this family of four people. They just come on. Play out their scenes. And then go off again. And that's it.

ACTRESS 1 And it's supposed to be inconclusive? Is that it? Or am I missing something as usual?

DIRECTOR No, that's the whole point. Its unfinished quality, its incompleteness —

ACTOR 2 Why?

DIRECTOR Why incomplete?

ACTOR 2 Yeah.

DIRECTOR Because that is the — condition — which the author gives us. Incomplete characters —

ACTOR 1 Look — sorry! I shouldn't have brought it up at all. It's just that I find this kind of — thing extremely —

DIRECTOR (*Obliging*) Please —

ACTRESS 1 Actually. What really gets *me* is the coincidence. It's a bit far-fetched, isn't it? That the one girl he should hire for sex turns out to be his own Stepdaughter? I mean to say —

ACTRESS 2 For God's sake, can't we just go and *do* it!

DIRECTOR All right. Thank you, everyone. Let me try to spell it out again. OK? What we have here is a series of extraordinary scenes. (*Indicating each* ACTOR *in turn*) A Father, a Stepdaughter. A Mother, his wife, and their son. That's it. We don't know where they come from. We don't know how they get to here. They're just here. They play out these violent, intimate scenes between themselves. The lights go down on them. And that's it. Finito.

ACTRESS 1 Of course she could have engineered it, couldn't she? The Stepdaughter? She could have set it up so that *she* would be the prostitute waiting. Knowing the client was her own Stepfather, like. No?

DIRECTOR Look. You're terrific. What you've been doing so far is absolutely right.

ACTRESS 1 Really? Do you really mean it?

DIRECTOR Just trust the lines. OK?

ACTRESS 1 I feel so — off — somehow —

ACTOR 1 I have to say I've never known a family the like of this one —

ACTRESS 2 Every family I've ever known is like this one. Including my own.

DIRECTOR From the beginning, please — thank you!

ASM (*Directions*) 'She is seated in the room. He enters the room behind her.'

Complete concentration. ACTOR 1 *leaps up, takes his place behind* ACTRESS 1 *who is seated. He is the elderly sex-client, she the experienced young tart. As they play, the screen at the back lights up. Moving/slide images of the Family, as before, but this time they are facing camera and us. We watch as they come nearer and nearer on the screen, walking the same road, as before. On stage, the only one facing the screen is the* ASM. *She eventually gets to her feet and points at what is happening on screen, but not before some of the following scene is played out.*

ACTOR 1   (*Rehearsal: prancing forward*) Good afternoon, miss.

ACTRESS 1   Hah? Oh. Good afternoon. (*Pause*) Sir.

ACTOR 1   You're very — inexperienced, aren't you?

ACTRESS 1   (*Knowing*) Oh, yes, sir. Very inexperienced, sir. Yes, sir.

ACTOR 1   It's your first time, isn't it? To do something like this?

ACTRESS 1   Oh, yes, sir, the first time, sir.

ACTOR 1   Never been here before? In this place?

ACTRESS 1   No, never.

ACTOR 1   Good. What I mean is you mustn't be afraid.

ACTRESS 1   (*Not a bit of it*) I'm very afraid, sir.

ACTOR 1   (*Pretend care*) You mustn't be afraid. I'll take care of everything. Do you understand? But you must do everything I tell you. You must obey me. In every particular. Is that understood? Everything I say!

ACTRESS 1   Yes, sir.

The image of the Family on the screen is now fixed, all six figures staring out at us, life-size. The ASM *is on her feet, looking at the screen. She points, dumbly.*

ACTOR 1   (*To* DIRECTOR) Do you think he should sort of — touch her somewhere there? I have this feeling. Not, you know? Just a slight — touch. On the arm, maybe?

DIRECTOR   You're forecasting, again. You must not forecast. *We* may know these two are family. But the *audience* doesn't know that. To you, she's just a pro, a hooker. To be used. OK?

ASM   Look!

The projection screen is flown out and the Family is now standing on the thrust stage, facing us. The DIRECTOR *and* ACTORS *turn to look, following the* ASM's *direction and the whole group breaks apart at what they see, the* DIRECTOR *approaching the thrust stage.*

DIRECTOR What in the name of Christ is this? Who let you in here? (*To* ASM, *who shrugs*) Is this some kind of joke? Hey? We're in the middle of rehearsal here. Do you mind? They're actually in costume, for Godsakes! OK. What's this? You, there —

Led by the FATHER, *the Family steps forward on the thrust stage,* MOTHER *and* SMALL CHILDREN *very close together,* STEPDAUGHTER *and* SON *to either side.*

FATHER We've come here, mister, looking for an author.

DIRECTOR What author?

FATHER That's immaterial — as a matter of fact. You see our author is dead, so, any author will do.

DIRECTOR Author? Who's this author you're talking about?

FATHER The same author as your own, mister.

DIRECTOR What're you talking about? We have no author here.

STEPDAUGHTER (*Leaping forward*) Hah! That's even better, so. We can start from scratch —

DIRECTOR Start from scratch what?

STEPDAUGHTER Your play —

DIRECTOR What play?

STEPDAUGHTER The play you're doing. We can finish it for you —

FATHER — completeness instead of incompleteness —

STEPDAUGHTER We are six! You are only four!

ACTRESS 2 They really are nuts!

ACTRESS 1 I think I'm going to faint —

ACTOR 2 (*Excitedly*) No! Listen! This is interesting!

FATHER But, still, we don't have any author round here, do we? (*To* DIRECTOR) Maybe you'd take on the job yourself, mister?

DIRECTOR Are you trying to be funny, by any chance?

FATHER Good God, man, no! What a thing to say. What we're going to give you is a drama of terrible suffering. Terrible suffering, indeed, yes —

STEPDAUGHTER (*Hysterical laugh*) Who knows? We might even make you a few bob!

FATHER That's enough from you now, miss! Let me handle this, now.

DIRECTOR You'll handle nothing! Just get out of here! Now!

FATHER Just a minute, now, just a minute —

DIRECTOR Out! Out! We've no time here for — lunatics!

FATHER Lunatics! That's very hurtful, mister, very hurtful indeed. To us, here. Very — insulting. You're an educated man, an intelligent man. I saw that the very first moment. That's educated there, I said. You know, and I know, how things in this life often seem peculiar. Mad! But they still tell us the truth. Know what I mean? But, of course you do. (*To rest of Family*) He understands our situation —

DIRECTOR No, I don't!

FATHER Oh, indeed you do. And I'll tell you why. If you were to dress up on the street and pretend to be someone else wouldn't they lock you up? And still isn't that how you actor people make a living?

DIRECTOR So we're the lunatics now, is that it?

FATHER No-no-no — All I'm trying to do is get you to see that what is made up is often truer than the real thing. Isn't that so? Don't you all spend your time here playing characters that are made up by somebody else?

DIRECTOR You make it sound like child's play. Well, let

me tell you something. Theatre is the only living art form left in this day and age. Why? Why, because it is the only true, human art form left, its instrument is the living human body of the actor, not some second-hand image from a machine. Yes, we let the great, classical characters of drama breathe and move and speak once more —

After a moment's pause ACTOR 1 *applauds loudly, shouting Bravo! Bravo! The other* ACTORS *smile among themselves and then, suddenly, the* FATHER *joins in the applause with great enthusiasm.*

FATHER Exactly! Exactly! Living beings! Maybe not real but more alive than the ordinary people walking the earth. I couldn't agree with you more.

DIRECTOR And a minute ago you were calling us lunatics —

FATHER No, mister. You were the one that called us lunatics. I was only talking about the acting, about theatricals.

DIRECTOR I see. Or, rather, I don't see.

FATHER Oh, you see well enough that each of us can be born into the world in different ways and different shapes. You can be born as a stone or a tree or a flower. Some are born as animals, some as water. And some of us are born as created characters, creatures who are imagined into existence. That's us.

The DIRECTOR *and* ACTORS *find this very funny.*

DIRECTOR So you're — created characters, is that right!

FATHER Yes. It's no laughing matter, I assure you. Quite the reverse. If you look at this woman and these children you'll see that they're in mourning. Everywhere we go we carry death with us. Now we're on stage again in this terrible drama. (*Claps his hands: a command*) Places!

At his command the members of the Family take up positions on the thrust stage, a series of tableaux: MOTHER *and* TWO SMALL CHILDREN *together;* STEPDAUGHTER, *back to us;* SON, *sunken to one side. The* FATHER *stands before them, his back to us, arms upraised like a conductor about to begin. Spectacular lighting change and music: perhaps a blackout and white spot on each figure in turn. Then back as before.*

Reaction to all this: ACTOR 1 *and* ACTRESS 1 *stand appalled,* ACTOR 2 *and* ACTRESS 2 *applaud,* DIRECTOR *is in a fury.* ASM *has her mouth open in amazement.*

DIRECTOR For Christsake, what's going on? Who's up in that lighting box? (*To* ASM) Will you get them to hell out of here before I go —

ASM All right! You must leave the theatre right now. Please!

ACTOR 1 You simply can't carry on like this in the theatre, you know.

ACTOR 2 I think they're great!

ACTRESS 1 This is beyond the beyond!

ACTOR 2 (*To* ACTRESS 2) Don't you think they're great?

DIRECTOR Out! Out!

FATHER Wait a minute —

DIRECTOR No — we've work to do here — work!

FATHER Work. I know about work. I've always got things done, you know. When I said so, people jumped to it. I know full well how you feel, mister. Time is money. It's only you're not used to this. Seeing characters that someone's invented jumping up on your stage like this. Strange, I grant you that. Speaking lines that aren't in your scripts there.

STEPDAUGHTER But we're still six characters — great characters at that — better bloody characters than you'd see in most plays, I can tell you. Only trouble is we're (*Pause*) unfinished —

FATHER (*Shout*) Do you mind, girl? (*To* DIRECTOR) As a matter of fact she's spoken the truth, for once in her life. Unfinished. That's the one word for us. I'd say — thrown in the waste-paper basket —

DIRECTOR In the what? What is this? — Unfinished?

FATHER Unfinished. You see, he imagined us into existence. And then stopped. In mid-air. It's our understanding, you see, that he gave up on us — For one reason or another he couldn't or wouldn't put us into a finished work of drama. We had been invented but never given form. We had been abused, mister, because once a character like us has been imagined, he can never die.

DIRECTOR I can't believe I'm having this conversation. (*Roar at* ASM) Who the hell turned on those stage lights!

ASM How do I know?

FATHER Once he imagined us we were there for good.

DIRECTOR Who the hell are you talking about?

FATHER The writer. Pirandello.

The ACTORS *immediately break into a huddled, excited, whispered argument between themselves. The* DIRECTOR *slowly joins them and the discussion continues, clearly with different views being expressed between them. The* ASM *is consulted and she rifles through her script — no help there — and the* FATHER *goes on as if nothing unusual has happened.*

He's dead now, though, isn't he? The great writer. Pirandello. Dust thou art — and all the rest of it. Not us, though. We go on and on. Once he put us down on the page we could never be blotted out again. (*The* DIRECTOR *has returned, thoughtfully, to the edge of the thrust stage*) You understand these things, mister. Tell us now — why do characters in books and plays never die? Why? Because they're not part of nature. Everything in nature has to die. But we're not part of nature as you people are. Its true nature allowed this man's mind to imagine us into existence. This is the way nature creates beings who are beyond nature herself! And that's why we're *more* real. (*Pointing*) Than you. And you! Or you! And you, there!

DIRECTOR (*Very quietly*) Why are you here?

FATHER We need to breathe once again. We need to play it all out again.

DIRECTOR You mean you want to join rehearsals? Is that it?

FATHER No, mister. We don't rehearse. You're the ones who have to rehearse. Not us.

ACTRESS 1 He said Pirandello. I distinctly heard him say Pirandello!

ACTOR 1 Do you mean they're going to do the same play as we are? On the same stage? Why, this is preposterous!

ACTRESS 1 I think we should all get out of here. At once.

ACTOR 1 No! No! That's the one thing we mustn't do! This is our stage. We must never surrender it. Ever!

ACTRESS 2 He said something else as well. He said they were 'imagined'.

ACTRESS 1 They simply have to be some kind of — escapees. Or something.

ACTOR 1 (*To* DIRECTOR) Well? Aren't you going to do something about it?

DIRECTOR Look. Just try to be patient, would you? Of course I'll deal with it.

ACTOR 2 Yeah! Let's go with it. It's a terrific idea! It'd make a great exercise! (*To* STEPDAUGHTER) Hey! You want to come down here beside me? (*She ignores him*)

ACTOR 1 Exercise! Exercise! Good God, what next?

ASM (*To* DIRECTOR) Do you want me to take notes?

DIRECTOR Not just now, not just now —

ACTRESS 2 Can we not get back to our proper script? *Please!*

FATHER But that's the point! You don't need a script. The whole drama is here! Locked inside the six of us. Waiting to burst out of us.

STEPDAUGHTER (*Leaping forward, wild, maniacal*) Bursting out of us! Bursting open! The way I burst open for him!

> *What follows is a rapid, violent moment, so quick that everyone else has scarcely time to react. She grabs the* FATHER *in the crotch with a wild laugh and quickly turns her back on him. He, in turn, spins her around again and slaps her across the face, once, twice, three times, becoming, almost at once, guilt-stricken and ashamed.*

FATHER (*Slapping her*) Don't laugh — don't laugh — mustn't laugh, mustn't, do you hear! (*Trying to hold her but she twists away from him*) — I'm sorry, lovey, I'm sorry — what's come over me! I shouldn't have — sorry, sorry —

STEPDAUGHTER (*Through tears of pain and rage and humiliation*) Ladies and Gentlemen! I will perform for you. I'm very good at performing —

ACTOR 1 (*Hopeful recognition*) Ah! It's that sort of play, is it?

FATHER Oh, what have I done! What have I done! Evil, evil, that's what I am —

> *The* STEPDAUGHTER *performs her song: 'Summertime'. Reaction:* ACTOR 1 *is impressed while*

ACTOR 2 *applauds loudly,* ACTRESS 1 *sinks into a seat and covers her face in her hands while* ACTRESS 2 *consults her script.*

ACTOR 1   Well, I must say she can sing alright.

DIRECTOR   (*To* FATHER) Listen here. This is horrible. We can't have carry-on like this, you know.

FATHER   Oh, I know it, mister. I feel completely ashamed of myself. I do. I do.

DIRECTOR   And the girl? What's wrong with her? Is she nuts?

FATHER   It's ten times worse than that, mister. If only she were mad —

STEPDAUGHTER   Sure! Infinitely worse than being nuts, if the truth be told, if it ever is — Know why? Because if I were only mad I wouldn't know anything. And I know everything. That's why I will run away at the end, you see. You want to see me run away? Well, then let's act it out. Now! All of it! Then! Just at the moment when this little darling here — (*Pause. To* LITTLE GIRL) Isn't she beautiful? She never speaks but she's beautiful, my beautiful, beautiful, dead little sister! I run away, you see, when she — (*To* LITTLE BOY) As for this lummox! Will you look at him! Oh, God! What a silly, silly, silly boy! To think he'd take a gun in his hand like that and —! Can you credit it? A gun! Where would a child find a gun in this country, I ask you? A gun! (*Desperately, to* DIRECTOR) Please! We must do it! Now! I can't wait — the freedom of it! Just to get away! From this hell-hole of a family or what will be left of it! In the end. (*Toward* SON) Away from him! Look at that hate on his face there! He hates us, you see. We are the second family. (*Goes and kisses the* MOTHER) He hates Mother here, you know. Though she won't accept it. He thinks she's dirty, you see. We are her dirt! Every time he looks at us he sees her in the bed with that other man, our father —

MOTHER Stop it! Stop it, do you hear! (*To* DIRECTOR) At least for the sake of the innocent children there —!

She suddenly collapses in a heap.

FATHER Get a chair for her.

ACTRESS 2 She's only fainted. I'll get something from the dressing room —

FATHER No-no-no! A chair! Just go and get her a chair!

DIRECTOR A chair! Get her a chair!

In some confusion the chair is produced and the MOTHER *is seated, the* FATHER *standing over her. He tries to lift the veil over her face but she stops him.*

MOTHER No — no — please —

FATHER Let them see your face —

MOTHER No!

FATHER (*Savagely*) Let them see your bloody face!

ACTRESS 2 Don't treat her like that! Look at the way he's treating her.

But the FATHER *has lifted the veil over the* MOTHER's *hat. Her face is a painted mask (actual or suggested) of extreme suffering, at any rate unrealistic in relation to every other face on stage. She rises and asserts herself for the first time.*

MOTHER (*To* DIRECTOR) Don't let him, sir, don't let this man do it. It's horrible, what he wants to put us through over and over again, please don't let him, sir —

FATHER Just listen to her!

DIRECTOR Just a minute. I don't get this at all. Is this

woman your wife?

FATHER   She is.

DIRECTOR   Well, how come so that she's dressed as a widow? Isn't she?

ACTOR 2 *gives a loud guffaw and everyone turns on him, in surprise, anger or warning, as the case may be.*

ACTRESS 2   What the hell are you laughing at?

ACTOR 2   Oh, for — It's only a performance!

FATHER   No, mister, that's where you're wrong. This isn't a performance. This is her story. This woman, my wife, went with another man. (*The* MOTHER *weeps and gathers the two children to her*) That man should be brought here. Right now!

MOTHER   No — no — please — no —

STEPDAUGHTER   He's dead, you monster — you —

DIRECTOR   Dead?

STEPDAUGHTER   Yes. That's why we're still in mourning.

FATHER   A mourning to last for ever —

STEPDAUGHTER   (*Tears*) Monster! Monster!

FATHER   Oh, yes, monster indeed. Well, let me tell you something about this suffering woman. Why isn't that man here? Because he's dead? No. Even if he's dead he could be brought here. That's not the reason. The reason is she never loved! She didn't love two men. She couldn't give herself to love. She just lay back. And conceived. One man, one son. Another man, two daughters and one son —

MOTHER   (*Almost in wonder at what she is saying*) All that is true — it's the loneliness of women —

FATHER   And what about the loneliness of men?

MOTHER   (*To* DIRECTOR) Sir, he made me do terrible things. He forced me, forced me to go away with that man —

STEPDAUGHTER   (*Rounding on her*) That's not true — of Daddy —

28

MOTHER It's true.

STEPDAUGHTER It's not true — not true — You loved Daddy!

MOTHER What can you know about it?

STEPDAUGHTER (*To* DIRECTOR) She's lying! I know her tricks. (*Pointing to* SON) It's because of him. That son of hers. Every day of her life she suffers at the way he's cut himself off from her. And now she's trying to reach him. With this lie. If she could only persuade him that she didn't abandon him — that it wasn't her fault he was left without a mother —

MOTHER (*Pointing to* FATHER) He forced me out of our house! I swear to it by Almighty God! Make him say it! Make him say it before my son here!

For the first time, the SON *comes alive, rising from a kind of stupor. He makes a few tentative steps toward the* MOTHER *and stops again.*

STEPDAUGHTER All I know is that we were happy together with Daddy. You can't deny it. Do you deny it? We were happy! Weren't we happy? (*Suddenly turning on the* LITTLE BOY, *shaking him*) Why don't you speak up, you little fool? Say we were happy when Dad was alive! Say it, can't you!

MOTHER Leave the child alone! I'd never say a word against your father. All I'm saying is that it wasn't my fault that I had to leave my first family, my own house and son — And that's the gospel truth.

Pause.

FATHER (*Loudly*) What she's saying is true! It was all my doing!

General shocked reaction to this. The Family

freezes in place and the Company begins to drift about.

ACTOR 1 Did you ever in your life see the like of that?

ACTRESS 2 That poor, poor woman —

ACTRESS 1 Are we or are we not proceeding with rehearsal? I'm merely asking a simple question —

DIRECTOR Just watch this for a moment, OK?

ACTRESS 1 I've watched quite enough of it, thank you very much.

DIRECTOR Just a few more minutes. I'm sure we can use it — I'm sure of it.

ACTRESS 1 Another of his enthusiasms!

ACTOR 2 (*To* DIRECTOR) Do you want us to do a scene or something with them? Now?

DIRECTOR No — no — Stay right where you are.

At this point, the DIRECTOR *acts as if he's directing the Family on the thrust stage, testing angles of sight, jumping up on the stage to reposition individuals etc. When the* SON *begins to move, prowling about the thrust stage, the whole Family becomes animated once again.*

SON (*Manic, almost to himself*) Confession time! My father is now going to confess. And we must all be prepared to forgive! Hah! He's now going to tell us about his great appetite for experience. How he can't stop himself. How he craves expiation —

FATHER (*Grabbing him*) Stoppit or I'll break your —

SON Go on! Hit me with all these people watching —

FATHER You don't believe in anything, do you? An empty, useless cur, that's what you are. (*Turning to* DIRECTOR) You see, mister, how he turns my very own words on me. The few words I have, to try to tell about my own terrible weaknesses —

DIRECTOR Very good, keep going, just keep going —

	don't explain —
SON	Words! Words!
FATHER	Yes, words. It's all we have. They're a help when we don't understand what's happening to us, when the devil takes us —
SON	The devil, now! Hoh! It wasn't you at all! Oh, no, the devil!
FATHER	(*Quietly to himself*) When I can talk about it, words bring me a little peace.
STEPDAUGHTER	And get rid of your guilt, no doubt?
FATHER	Nothing'll ever get rid of that —
STEPDAUGHTER	Not even the money?
FATHER	What money? What're you talking about, girl?
STEPDAUGHTER	(*Mocking*) I'm a self-made man! I owe nothing to anyone and never have! I've paid my way — Well, you paid your way when you turned me into a whore!

There is general consternation at this and the SON *confronts the* STEPDAUGHTER.

SON	You little — little — little — exhibitionist! There was no need to bring that up in public —
STEPDAUGHTER	Go to hell! That foul woman's shop. He left the blue envelope on the small table in the back room. Fifteen pounds in fivers, a lot of money —
ACTOR 1	What does she mean? A lot of money? When exactly was all this?
STEPDAUGHTER	Madame Pace. The finest women's — apparel. The latest styles —
MOTHER	(*Cry*) I thought she was a decent woman, God forgive me —
DIRECTOR	Just a moment, this woman, this Madame Pace, who is she?
STEPDAUGHTER	You mean you've never heard of her?
MOTHER	Her name was in the paper, sir.
FATHER	They turfed her out of the country, in the end. You must have heard of her?

STEPDAUGHTER But not before he came to the shop, his tongue hanging out for it —

DIRECTOR But where exactly was this shop?

MOTHER In the city, sir.

DIRECTOR But where did she come from, this Madame Pace?

MOTHER No one ever knew, sir.

FATHER She came out of the war.

ACTOR 1 The war? What war?

FATHER (*Impatiently*) The War! The War!

> *There is a definite, sharp, shocked pause. The Family look at one another, the DIRECTOR and ACTORS look at one another: bewilderment, even a little fear.*

DIRECTOR All right! All right! We'll sort this out later. Just keep going, keep going.

> *This is exactly what the Family does, as if switched on again by his command.*

SON (*To Family*) You've no self-respect! Any of you! Parading yourselves like this. It's disgusting, that's what it is. And you! (*Stepdaughter*) Anything so that you can — display yourself, that's it, isn't it? Fifteen pounds. Why don't you tell the full truth? That he never had to pay it? That he had no reason to pay it?

STEPDAUGHTER How do you know? Were you there? Maybe you were there. Hiding in the room. Watching while I stripped. You horrible thing!

MOTHER Oh, you shameless, shameless —

STEPDAUGHTER Shame? I don't feel a bit of shame. Know what I feel? Desire. I feel this thrilling desire, to act out that scene again, that back room, the dark, the old furniture, the blue envelope on the little table. I go behind the screen. I begin to take off my clothes, for him —

FATHER (*To* DIRECTOR) Mister, you've got to stop her. The way she's telling it it's all wrong, simply wrong —

STEPDAUGHTER Of course! It's wrong, is it? Hah?

FATHER Of course —

STEPDAUGHTER And you're the only one who'll tell the truth, I suppose?

FATHER (*Roar*) Don't vex me, girl, I'll not be responsible!

STEPDAUGHTER (*Scream*) You've never been responsible! Ever! For anything! Except for destruction!

The DIRECTOR *leaps up on the thrust stage between them, the director-at-work.*

DIRECTOR All right, all right! Not so close to one another. Just move apart on that, would you? Thank you, if you could just step over — that's it. There! OK? Keep going, keep going —

He leaps back down to lower rehearsal area again.

FATHER (*Meditatively, almost to himself*) Words! We think we're all using the same words but we're not. Every man and woman has a different meaning to words that might be the same. It's the curse of Adam. (*Toward the* MOTHER) Look at this woman here. You wouldn't think it, would you now, that I've devoted my life with her to trying to make her happy?

MOTHER You threw me out of the house!

FATHER See what I mean? I threw her out of the house, I threw her out of the house, God Almighty!

MOTHER I can't tell things the way he tells them. He was always great at the talk. He could always bamboozle anyone with the talk. While all I ever wanted was to have simple things —

FATHER And that's why I married her! Wasn't that why I — loved you? The simple nature that you

33

had, how clear everything was for you, how simple and pure. (*The* MOTHER *shakes her head vigorously*) You see! I can't get through to her at all! Never could. Oh, yes, love, for her children. Never for me. Never! (*Ends in a sort of sob*)

STEPDAUGHTER Oh, clever, clever. Make him tell what his cleverness did to the rest of us!

FATHER Oh, the damage we do when we think we're doing our best!

ACTRESS 1 *suddenly throws down her script in anger.*

ACTRESS 1 I'm sorry — I've really had quite enough of this — are we or are we not proceeding with rehearsal — ?

ACTOR 2 This is rehearsal, for Godsakes — What do you think it is?

DIRECTOR Look. I just want to hear this out. OK? I think we might be able to use it. Maybe — Maybe not —

ACTRESS 2 (*Toward the* FATHER) Well, do we have to listen to that fellow all the time? Why not let the women speak more?

DIRECTOR (*To* FATHER) Right. Try to play down your — opinions. Just tell us your story. You know. Straight.

FATHER Well — I dunno. I've made my pile. What's wrong with that? We've always had everything we wanted. Maybe that's not true either. It's very confusing to me now. There was this man. A partner of mine. Well, not a partner. A director of one of my — well, he was a class of a secretary. In one of the offices. (*The* MOTHER *begins to weep*) Look at her! She's already crying for him. He was an inoffensive sort of a man, mister. The same as her. I knew they'd never do anything bad between them. So, I let them alone a lot —

STEPDAUGHTER Then he thought up something bad for them himself! He made them do it!

FATHER That's a terrible way of putting it. I thought it was best for everyone. The two of them. Me, too. I couldn't stand watching the two of them together. The looks they gave one another. Whispers. I went around like an animal in the house. I thought — as God is my judge — I might kill someone. Maybe myself. If I didn't take steps, that is —

DIRECTOR Why didn't you sack this guy?

FATHER I did! But then I had to watch her — the poor creature! She dwindled away in front of my eyes. I couldn't stand it. It was worse than having a disease myself —

MOTHER But my —

FATHER (*Quickly cutting her off*) Your son! Isn't that what you were going to say? About your son — I know it!

MOTHER Yes, my son. Long before any of this he took my son from me.

FATHER Notice the way she puts it! 'Took my son from me' — her words!

MOTHER Yes!

FATHER No! That wasn't the way it was! When the boy was small she couldn't cope! She moped and wept day and night. And the boy was suffering! What could I do but find someone else to mind him? To give him a normal life.

STEPDAUGHTER Normal! Will you look at him now!

FATHER It's not my fault he's the way he is. My motive was right. What else can I say? Motive, that's what matters, your motive. Tried to do right. I did. Always tried to do right. I'm cursed with this constant need to interfere, to improve things, like — around me. Small things, big things. Organize them, like. I'll pay anything to better it. Life won't let me, though! (STEP-DAUGHTER *erupts into wild, hysterical laughter*)

Stop her! Stop her, someone! I can't stand it, the way she laughs, I'm going to —

DIRECTOR Quiet! (*She stops at once*) Go on — Tell your story —

FATHER I came to hate her, mister. (*To* MOTHER) Hate her. The suffering of it —

MOTHER And he sent me away.

FATHER Well provided for. Both of them. Him and her. That they could live as husband and wife. Where no one would know them. I knew the terrible thing I was doing. And why? Freedom! Freedom from me, you see. And I never lost touch with them. In case they'd ever want, you see. To help. If needs be. And always money in the post for them. But he kept changing — their — abode. No sooner had I caught up with them than he'd switch addresses again. He seemed to have this queer notion about my — interest. Which was pure as the driven snow, mister, as God is my — And over the years I watched this little family grow. With love. With tenderness — (*To* STEP-DAUGHTER) She remembers that —

STEPDAUGHTER Oh, I remember it! He appeared outside the school gate. He said I had nice pigtails and I showed off my dress. He watched me grow, a strange man in a raincoat —

FATHER 'Man in a —!' That's scandalous, scandalous, so it is, the way she puts it —

STEPDAUGHTER Oh! Is it now!

FATHER (*To* DIRECTOR) I'll take your advice, mister. I'll not be baited. Tell the story! Story. Empty house. She had filled my house with suffering but she had filled it! And now she was gone — and the boy, when he came home to me, was no longer my son. What had I done? What had I done? I was frantic again but this time it was different. I had to know all about their little family. I was now spending all my days following them, seeing their ordinary every-day life. Was she happy now?, I asked myself. Had she stopped her moping and her crying and her humours? These were the questions. And the little girl would come out the school gate —

STEPDAUGHTER And he'd follow me down the street. I used to look back at him. Like this. Teasing. I used to think, I'll fool him. And when I'd reach the front door I'd wave. Like this. She never reported him, Mother. She knew damn well who he was. Just took me out of school for a few days. But when I got back, there he was again. Changed schools. The same thing. There he was. At the school gates. How was it he wasn't caught? Then one day he gave me a straw hat. Out of an old brown paper bag. It was my first hat.

Long pause.

DIRECTOR Hmm. Very interesting, but this wouldn't really work, would it? On stage, I mean —

FATHER But this is only leading up to the real drama —

SON (*Sneer*) The real drama!

FATHER (*Fury*) The real drama, the real drama — be-sides, as you can see, mister, she's no longer that little schoolgirl now, is she?

STEPDAUGHTER With her little knickers showing —

SON You're disgusting, so you are —

FATHER God Almighty, what is to become of us!

STEPDAUGHTER You know perfectly well what is to become of us! You know well how this has to end!

FATHER Story — story — story — (*Pause, finding the story*) They disappeared, mister.

DIRECTOR Disappeared? The family?

FATHER Overnight. To this day I don't know where he had them hid. Another town, maybe.

STEPDAUGHTER (*Hysterical*) My father died —

FATHER   But not before he hid them away somewhere from me —

STEPDAUGHTER   From you?

FATHER   From me. I gave up everything. For days, for months, for years I searched for them, lost woman, lost children, spent a fortune, not important, would have spent two fortunes. No sign or trace of them —

STEPDAUGHTER   (*Lost*) My father died my father died my father died —

FATHER   It was then — I say this before every witness here present and I ask your pardon for it — it was then I began to whore.

MOTHER   In front of the children!

FATHER   They have to hear. All must hear. I am not, in this way, what you'd call a bad man. Woman! Such a need for a woman. Constant. And not one of them would look at me twice because of what I carried in my face. But I could pay, you see. And I learned how to pay. And I learned about all the other men who paid. Respectable suits. The dignity of man! But we're all like that. Only some have the courage to talk about it —

STEPDAUGHTER   Courage? Is it courage to do such awful things?

FATHER   Courage to talk about them!

STEPDAUGHTER   I've had enough of this! Why are you all listening to him? (*To* ACTRESSES) Why are you women listening? You know full well what he's doing, what they always do. Slithering out of it. Men! Animals! But that's all right, oh, that's all right as long as they say they're sorry for it all. The women have to pick up the pieces! Everyone in bits. Sorry! Lives destroyed. Sorry — sorry. Men saying — sorry!

DIRECTOR   We're getting off the track again, somehow — Could we just go back to —

ACTOR 1   Are we supposed to act all this? I really am quite confused.

FATHER (*Loud roar*) How could I know that when that man died they were destitute and in the clutches of that woman Madame Pace?

A long pause.

DIRECTOR And this — Madame Pace — she ran a brothel?

FATHER A brothel? A brothel?

STEPDAUGHTER She ran a shop.

DIRECTOR To sell sex?

MOTHER She sold clothes, the most beautiful clothes you've ever seen.

DIRECTOR And you (*Father*) came there. For sex?

FATHER I confess!

DIRECTOR (*To* STEPDAUGHTER) And you were the girl that was offered to him? In this — shop?

MOTHER How could I know — that dirty woman when she offered me the sewing for the few shillings — that it was my daughter she had her eyes on —!

STEPDAUGHTER (*Hysterical*) Isn't that some scene! To put on your stage. What a drama that'd be in the theatre! Father and Stepdaughter in that dark little back room —

FATHER But the mother walked in on them —

STEPDAUGHTER But not in time to stop it —

FATHER (*Breathlessly*) In time! In time —

STEPDAUGHTER Liar!

FATHER (*Panting, very rapidly*) Besides. He knows who she is. Right away. The Father. He knows. Shocked. She is nearly naked but he recognizes her, see, knows who she is. His — stepdaughter. Why wouldn't he!

Long pause: surfacing, surprised at himself.

Of course, I did —

STEPDAUGHTER (*Tears*) Liar! Liar!

39

FATHER   (*Complete change: composed, matter-of-fact*) Do you know something? I can explain it like this. We all think that we're one person. But we're not. It's the greatest illusion in life. Tragic. We're not one person at all. Each of us is made of many persons. We're one thing to one person, another thing to someone else. Know what I mean? And when we're caught in the act — it's like being suspended — in mid-air. And then we see that all of us wasn't in the shameful thing we were doing at all. Only part of us. That's why it's such a terrible injustice to be judged on that one action alone. Do you see what I mean? You see she surprised me in that one act. She never lets me forget it. Never will. This is the nub of it all. Justice. It also makes it very interesting drama, doesn't it? This particular aspect? Very interesting to act on stage. (*Short pause: points to* SON) Then there's him!

SON   I've nothing to do with any of this!

FATHER   Oh, yes you do —

SON   Leave me alone! I want no part of any of you —

STEPDAUGHTER   Because we're dirt. Isn't that it? Well, let me tell you, she's your mother as well. Or do you want to deny that?

SON   You're disgusting —

STEPDAUGHTER   Is that so? Listen to this! I want to be disgusting. I really do. Just to watch that look on your face — twisted, sick —

SON   A public spectacle —

FATHER   Stop it! Both of you!

SON   No! There is something else. What hasn't been said before now. How she (*Stepdaughter*) tried to blackmail him (*Father*).

DIRECTOR   When was this?

STEPDAUGHTER   Lies! Lies!

SON   One fine day, the two of us alone in the house, him and me, one at one end of the house, one at the other, she (*Stepdaughter*) came to the front door, this painted tramp, she asked for him by name. I'd no idea who she was. Everyone on the street watching. Then another day, back she came again, this time with that little girl there, holding hands, like beggars, only insolent. Then another day, back she came again, I heard her at the door, demanding money, I saw him give it to her —

FATHER (*Loudly, anguished*) I owed it to them! I owed it to the mother there —

SON How did I know any of that? I knew nothing about them! I didn't know they existed. Then, another day, they all arrived on the doorstep, out of the blue —

FATHER Destitute! Destitute!

SON All like tinkers, and he said to me, 'This is your mother, too!' This is your family now! (*Weeping*) I can't tell you what I felt. I can't tell you what I feel now. I am only a half person. I am — unfinished — I don't want to be in this —

FATHER What're you talking about? You're just what you are, nothing more, nothing less.

SON (*Violently*) What do you know about it? What do you know about me? Nothing!

FATHER (*Abject*) All that's true, too true. I can't know him, mister, can't know my own son. (*Brightening, to* DIRECTOR) But doesn't that make it even better for the stage? The way the son cuts himself off. The mother coming back, seeing him for the first time for years, hardly recognizing him but knowing full well that this is her son! Marvellous drama! But, no, he won't have anything to do with her. (*Pointing*) Look at the way she's crying, now —

STEPDAUGHTER The bloody fool that she is!

FATHER (*To* DIRECTOR, *about the Son*) Funny thing, you know. He says he has no part in it when, in fact, the whole thing revolves around him, in a way. The mother. Even the two kids. Look at the little boy, there, scared out of his wits. Made to feel unwanted in the house. By him! (*Points to* SON) He has treated the whole family in an awful way since they came back. That poor little boy, there. You know that child reminds me of his dead father, always trying to hide, humble, never saying anything —

DIRECTOR I don't think we want to use the two kids, you've no idea the problems kids cause on stage —

FATHER No problem, no problem. They're gone almost immediately. The little girl is the first to die. Then him.

DIRECTOR Good — good. I think we've got the makings of something here —

STEPDAUGHTER But who's going to be the leading character in it?

FATHER Will you shut up, you!

DIRECTOR And it's a new angle, a new angle — Tell me. Have you ever acted on stage yourself?

FATHER Oh, no, mister, never acted any more than anyone acts in their daily life.

DIRECTOR Ha-ha! Well. We still don't have an author —

FATHER Why don't you do it yourself, mister?

DIRECTOR What!

FATHER You could do the writing yourself. Why not?

DIRECTOR Because I've never written a thing in my life, that's why not —

FATHER You could do it!

DIRECTOR Oh, come on!

FATHER There's nothing to it. Sure, isn't everyone writing nowadays. And you'll always have us six there, to act it out, scene by scene.

DIRECTOR But we still need someone to actually get it down on paper.

FATHER (*Toward* ASM) But she can do that —

ASM I'm game to have a go —

FATHER There we are!

DIRECTOR Its potential is very — OK! Just come backstage. We'll work it out.

ASM And me?

DIRECTOR Of course, of course, let's go —

FATHER All six of us, mister?

DIRECTOR What? Yes, all six.

He begins to lead the SIX and ASM off into the wings, stops, sees the ACTORS still standing below the thrust stage.

We'll take a break, shall we? Back in twenty minutes, everyone! OK? Twenty minutes —

ASM Twenty minutes call!

She follows the DIRECTOR and the others off. The ACTORS look at one another.

ACTOR 1 Good — (*Pause*) — God!

ACTRESS 1 Can he actually be serious, do you think?

ACTOR 1 Never seen the like. And I've seen a *lot*.

ACTRESS 2 (*To ACTOR 2*) Go for coffee? We've time to go across the road.

ACTRESS 1 It is, if I may say so, the end.

ACTOR 2 The end? The end? It's not the end, it's the beginning! It may be exactly what we need. A bit of reality in what we're doing instead of this half-baked — (*Script in hand. To ACTRESS 2*) Come on, let's go —

They go.

ACTOR 1 (*Following more slowly with ACTRESS 1*) Never much liked these directors who want to be writers — What about you?

ACT TWO

Lights up. The stage is now partially set, very basic setting, flats, door, shop-window, sofa, for the MADAME PACE *scene; fountain, bushes, trees for the garden scene of Part Two of the play.*

The DIRECTOR *and* ASM *lead on the six family members from one side,* FATHER *followed by* MOTHER *with the two small children clutching her knees, followed by* STEPDAUGHTER, *with the* SON *straggling behind. The* ASM *is carrying a small cassette recorder.*

At the same time, the four ACTORS *stroll on from the other side and the two groups confront each other.*

DIRECTOR   (*To* ASM) This looks very promising. When we get going I want you to record all their dialogue! Have you got the cassettes? Then we can use the stuff later with the company.

ASM   Should I make notes of their moves?

DIRECTOR   Don't bother. We'll find the real blocking later with the actors. (*Toward* ACTORS) Ah, there they are! We're all set and ready to go at this end. You people all right? Good. Now. (*To* FATHER, *indicating set*) Take a look at the set, would you? — What you want, is it?

FATHER   And where's the fountain?

DIRECTOR   Over there.

FATHER   And Madame Pace's shop, where's the small back room? Behind the shop?

DIRECTOR   (*Taking in the space*) We'll have that somewhere about — here —

STEPDAUGHTER   (*Wail*) But it's not a bit like what it was!

DIRECTOR   Obviously there'll be adjustments as we go along —

FATHER   You're going to have to have a mirror.

DIRECTOR (*To* ASM, *who makes note*) Mirror.

FATHER A cheval mirror. Very beautiful. Over there.

STEPDAUGHTER And a little table — for the blue envelope. With the money that he (*Father*) brought with him. To pay me.

FATHER And a screen. Standing about here.

STEPDAUGHTER For me. To take my clothes off. Behind it.

FATHER Clothes! Of course. Clothes hangers, clothes. There has to be a rail of clothes, all kinds of clothes, hats, coats. Garments. (*Awkwardly*) Underthings. For Madame Pace —

DIRECTOR We can't have everything right away, you know, first time round —

STEPDAUGHTER (*High*) That sofa! It's all wrong! Wrong colour, wrong size. It should be yellow, very — plush, a sort of floral pattern, loose covers, a bit ripped at the back —

FATHER We must have clothes hangers, a rail. Plus the small table. Large mirror.

DIRECTOR (*Extreme patience*) All right! All right! For heavensakes. (*To* ASM) Look. See what you can do, would you mind — It's just to dress the bloody place a bit. OK? Eternally grateful —

ASM goes off. She will come back with stagehands carrying the various items during the following.

STEPDAUGHTER Nothing is like what it was, nothing —

DIRECTOR Look, this is a stage! A stage! We're in the business of creating things. Do you understand? Making theatre. Not reconstructing something.

STEPDAUGHTER (*Wandering about, lost*) All wrong, all wrong —

FATHER (*Drawing himself up, centre, very loudly*) I am ready! To begin!

He gestures to the MOTHER, SON *and* CHILDREN *to stand aside, which they do, as the* ASM *and stagehands complete the furnishing.*

DIRECTOR (*To* ACTORS) You've all been very, very patient. Much appreciated. Now. We'll record the dialogue, of course. But what I want you to do is pick up as much as you can. Rough copy, if you follow me.

ACTRESS 1 Do you mean — *improvise?*

DIRECTOR No-no-no. Relax! You don't have to improvise, I assure you. Believe me, when you actually see them it'll be plain sailing. It's going to be quite extraordinary. Like taking something off the street.

ACTOR 2 Oh, great!

ACTOR 1 But what are we supposed to be doing? I mean, right now?

DIRECTOR Well, for the moment just stand and watch. We can figure out the details later on. This is just a rehearsal. With this crowd doing the rehearsal for a change. OK?

FATHER (*Panic*) Just a moment, mister, if I've heard you right — did you say rehearsal?

DIRECTOR Yes, exactly, a rehearsal, and then the actors will pick it up and we'll get down to serious business —

FATHER And whàt, may I ask, is this rehearsal supposed to be about?

DIRECTOR Like any other rehearsal. To try things out. For the benefit of the actors there, what else — All right, everyone?

FATHER Rehearsals — but we can't have rehearsals, we're the actual characters —

DIRECTOR (*Humouring him*) Of course, of course — characters — Now, can we start?

FATHER It's the wrong word. Rehearsal.

DIRECTOR Look. Use whatever word you want. Rehearsal. Performance. Let's just get the material out into the open, shall we?

FATHER But we're the real characters.

DIRECTOR And *they* are the real actors! To play the characters on stage while the characters themselves stay in the script. Or should do, at any rate —

FATHER But you don't have any script.

DIRECTOR Are you trying to be funny again?

FATHER You're lucky to have live characters here to do it for you.

DIRECTOR But not to act, surely!

FATHER No. To do it as it really is.

DIRECTOR 'To do it as it really is!' And I suppose you're going to tell me that that would make superior theatre? Better than what we might produce?

FATHER Yes, mister.

The DIRECTOR *looks at the* ACTORS *and the* ACTORS *look at him before they all break out into laughter. Cries of 'Well, that's put it up to us!' 'At least we can retire', 'Isn't that something!'*

DIRECTOR Oh, God! This gets better and better. (*To* ACTORS) All right, you crowd. We know who's playing who already, don't we? Same as before, folks. You (*Actress 2*) stay with the Mother, again. Right? You know, I think it might help if we had a name for her —

FATHER Amalia.

DIRECTOR Amalia?

FATHER (*Pointing to* MOTHER) That's her name.

DIRECTOR But we can't use her real name —

FATHER (*Anxiously*) And what other name would you use? Though, if it's going to be this lady here, maybe, I dunno — It's very confusing, so it is. This one, that one, which one. I'm listening to myself talking. Whose voice is it? (*Rising panic*) I can hear myself talking! I hear this! I've never heard my voice before — what's come over me!

DIRECTOR It's all right — calm down, are you all right? It's nothing, sometimes happens to people on stage, hearing their own voice. Amalia,

47

	Amalia, so what? We don't need a name. What made me bring that up? You (*Actor 2*) stay with the Son. And you (*Actress 1*) stay with the Stepdaughter.
STEPDAUGHTER	Me?
DIRECTOR	No, her. (*Pointing to* ACTRESS 1)

The STEPDAUGHTER *screeches with hysterical laughter, enough to stop everyone in their tracks. She points at* ACTRESS 1.

STEPDAUGHTER	That — woman!
DIRECTOR	Cut it out, would you —
STEPDAUGHTER	(*Still in hysterics, half laughter, half tears*) Sorry —
ACTRESS 1	I've never been so — in all my life! The nerve! (*To other* ACTORS) Do you see what's going on? Absolutely! I'm finished with this! Finished with it!
DIRECTOR	No-no-no — Please! Leave it to me!
ACTRESS 1	Finished! Absolutely!
STEPDAUGHTER	Sorry, it wasn't you, it could have been anyone —
ACTRESS 1	'That woman', indeed!
STEPDAUGHTER	I wasn't thinking of you —
ACTRESS 1	You surprise me —
STEPDAUGHTER	(*Vehemently*) I was thinking of myself! Me! You're not me! You're not even a bit like me, so you're not!
FATHER	She's taken the words out of my mouth, mister. Exact words. Us. Look at us! You see us! The outside of us. Not the inside. You can't see our — (*Searches for the word*) — our — souls —
DIRECTOR	What is this? Souls! What next? This isn't a religious gathering, for Christsake, it's a theatre. A theatre! Outside, inside, no big deal. We see enough of you —
FATHER	But not our — souls —
DIRECTOR	Do you mind? Could we just cut out this soul-stuff? Let's just concentrate on the material.

All right? The material! What you people express is the material. And the actors here will give that material theatrical expression. Not any other kind of expression — theatrical expression. Do you follow me? Theatrical substance, theatrical form through the medium of their bodies, their voices, their gestures, and so on and so forth. Get me? There's nothing particularly spiritual about it. In fact it's very sensual, if the truth be told. Body work. Sweat. But! But! And this is what is so extraordinary. All this, the end product, can produce a magic unlike any other human activity in existence. (*Pause for effect*) What's more, my friends, these actors, these same actors have worked on far more — elevated — material in their time, far more —

ACTOR 1 *applauds loudly. The other* ACTORS *look: pleased, amused, embarrassed. The Family simply stare.*

FATHER (*Almost to himself*) We're — ourselves. We're the ones inside our own bodies. We're the ones who are — suffering —

DIRECTOR Look — you don't have to worry about the end-effect, it's just a matter of technique. That's all.

FATHER (*Outraged*) Technique! It's not like that at all.

DIRECTOR My friend. You're on a stage now. And on a stage one cannot exist as oneself. You cannot be yourself. He (*Actor 1*) is going to play you. And that's that. No discussion. Can we get back to the material now? Thank you!

FATHER It's just occurred to me. I can see it all now —

DIRECTOR See what now?

FATHER Why he wasn't able to put us into a play. He couldn't because he could only see us as living, suffering human beings. He couldn't

	see us as created characters. There was this line, you see, that he couldn't cross.
DIRECTOR	Who are you talking about?
FATHER	Pirandello.
DIRECTOR	You mustn't — you know — do this. You're — disturbing yourself like this. Why not just give us that story of yours? That's all. Your story. Like before. It was — terrific. It really was.
FATHER	And this gentleman here (*Actor 1*) is going to play me. Is that right?
ACTOR 1	Do you object?
FATHER	Oh, not at all. It's a great — honour, great honour. It's only, well, not to put a tooth in it — (*Struggling*) You won't be able to — able to —
ACTOR 1	Able to what?
FATHER	Inside me. Great — confusion, you see. Feelings going this way, that way. Terrible love, terrible hate. Unfinished, don't you know. And how do you finish someone who isn't finished? I ask you that. Besides. What are they going to say when they come to watch all this?
DIRECTOR	(*Heavy joke*) Oh-ho! Now he's worried about the critics! (*Uneasy laughter from the* ACTORS) Let's just concentrate on getting the play together first. Shall we? We'll open up the spaces here, everyone. Those not on — over to one side, please —
ASM	(*Notes*) 'Stepdaughter centre, Father by doorway.'
DIRECTOR	(*To* STEPDAUGHTER) Everything all right for you, is it?
STEPDAUGHTER	Nothing is right round here.
DIRECTOR	Good God, you didn't expect to find this Madame Whatsits' place down to the last button, now, did you?
FATHER	Pace —
STEPDAUGHTER	Madame Pace —
DIRECTOR	You said the place had wallpaper —

FATHER	White —
STEPDAUGHTER	Pink rose pattern.
DIRECTOR	Well, there's none of that here, is there? And it's no big deal, is it? (*To* ASM) Move the small table down a bit. What about that envelope?
ASM	I gave it to him (*Father*) —
FATHER	But it's not a blue envelope, mister.
DIRECTOR	Oh, you can imagine it's blue, can't you? Of course you can. So! Scene One. The Stepdaughter in the room. (ACTRESS 1 *quickly jumps up*) No-no-no not you. (*Toward* STEPDAUGHTER) Her! All you have to do is watch her. Closely.
STEPDAUGHTER	And see how I bring it alive!
ACTRESS 1	I'll bring it alive, never you fear, darling.
DIRECTOR	Now-now! Now-now! Please! Just a moment. I'd forgotten. The scene actually begins between you (*Stepdaughter*) and this Madame —
STEPDAUGHTER	Madame Pace!
DIRECTOR	We don't have her — ?
FATHER	She didn't come with us, you see.
DIRECTOR	Yes, but where is she?
FATHER	Oh, she's alive. The same as the six of us.
DIRECTOR	(*Uneasily looking*) Is she back there somewhere?
FATHER	Mister. (*Pointing to the two* ACTRESSES) Can I talk to them?
DIRECTOR	Who?
FATHER	Your two women there. Do you mind, ladies? I hope you don't — mind — now. But would you give me the loan of some of your clothes?
ACTRESS 1	Clothes! What is he talking about?
ACTRESS 2	Do you mean what we're wearing?
ACTRESS 1	Why doesn't he go to Wardrobe?
FATHER	Your clothes. Hat, maybe. Maybe a coat. Other things.
ACTRESS 1	What other things? He's a creep!
ACTRESS 2	(*Grabbing items from a chair*) Here you go! I've a coat and hat. But I want them back, mind. In one piece.

FATHER (*Very awkward*) Stockings —
ACTRESS 2 Sorry. Don't wear stockings.

> *Suddenly, everyone turns and looks at ACTRESS 1. She feels completely trapped. She turns her back on the whole company and, very slowly, hitches up her skirts and removes a pair of elegant stockings. She slowly passes them to ACTRESS 2 who, equally slowly, passes them to the DIRECTOR who, finally, passes them to the FATHER.*

FATHER (*Extremely embarrassed*) Other things.

> *Again all look toward ACTRESS 1 who, again, slowly turns her back on them. Uncertain pause. Then she slowly puts her hands up under sweater and takes off her bra. She passes this, as before, to ACTRESS 2, to DIRECTOR, to FATHER. The FATHER then goes to the clothes rack and arranges these items, with great dignity, on hangers on the rack.*

DIRECTOR Do you mind me asking? What exactly are you up to?
FATHER I'm making the place ready. For Madame Pace.

> *Light change. Music. He stands back. All the Family become rigid. The set door swings open and MADAME PACE steps in. She is dressed in a 1950s suit (power-suited for the day), the suggestion of money and style, a woman in middle age who looks older, a helmet of steel grey hair, a face ravaged and determined. The DIRECTOR and ACTORS instinctively step back. MADAME PACE walks to the rail of clothes, examining it. Then she looks at the STEPDAUGHTER, clicks her fingers and the STEPDAUGHTER runs meekly to her. MADAME PACE examines the girl, details of her body, the inside of her mouth and so on as if*

> *she were testing a piece of material. Then she nods and whispers something to her. The two of them walk back upstage whispering.*

DIRECTOR   What the hell —!

FATHER   Madame Pace, mister.

ACTRESS 1   Who is she? Do you know her?

ACTOR 2   Never saw her before in my life —

FATHER   But why are you surprised, ladies and gentlemen? Don't you believe in the power of your own place? Your stage? How it draws figures out of the shadows? Can't you see now that this is more real than you will ever be? (*Pointing*) You. And you. And you. Because it will be repeated, repeated, again and again, when you are all long dead and buried in your graves. And who, now, is going to play Madame Pace? No one. That's who. Because Madame Pace herself is here. Look at the way my stepdaughter recognized her! They draw closer together. Madame is examining her, testing her, because Madame knows her trade. It isn't everyone who measures up to the requirements of Madame Pace.

> MADAME PACE *and the* STEPDAUGHTER *are in close conversation, much explaining, gesticulating, questioning. The others watch them.*

ACTOR 1   Speak up, will you!

ACTOR 2   We can't hear a bloody thing.

ACTOR 1   Projection, please! Louder, louder —

STEPDAUGHTER   Louder, is it? What we're talking about isn't shouted in public! It was different when I shouted it at him (*Father*)! I was trying to disgrace him then. Not now. It has to be all whispers now. Otherwise Madame Pace'd end up in jail!

DIRECTOR   Well, I've news for you, young lady, this isn't

any public place, it's a theatre and a stage and we're trying to rehearse and if you don't speak up no one will hear you — We're standing beside you and we can't hear a thing. Just think of what it'd be like if we had an audience out there! OK? Let's just take a deep breath, again, shall we, and start over. Just pretend. Pretend we're not here. You're all alone with Madame — ah-there, chatting. Clear speech, please. Both of you. (STEPDAUGHTER, *sly grin, shakes her head*) Why not?

STEPDAUGHTER There's someone else might hear —

DIRECTOR Good God! You're not going to spring someone else on us, are you!

FATHER She means me, mister.

DIRECTOR You!

FATHER I'm behind the door there —

DIRECTOR You're-behind-the-door? Well, for Christsake go get behind the door, then! (*Which the* FATHER *does*) On with it.

STEPDAUGHTER (*Suddenly beaten*) She's saying I have to do this. Or she won't give my mother any more money.

MADAME PACE (*Accent*) I do not say he is an old fool, which he is. I say he is a clean old man. Also he is — careful.

STEPDAUGHTER (*Dully*) Very careful. He will not ask many things. Ten minutes.

ACTOR 1 What sort of accent was that?

ACTRESS 1 Where is she from?

DIRECTOR (*To* MADAME PACE) That the way you normally speak? You do know English, don't you?

MADAME PACE I know sufficient. English. Also I know many other languages.

DIRECTOR I see. Well. That's actually good. What I mean is a mix of sex, foreign woman, good. Never fails to work. Great. Great!

STEPDAUGHTER (*Hysteria*) Great! Great? Of course it's great. Sounds great in broken English, doesn't it? 'Ten minutes. Old man. Very careful.'

MADAME PACE Not so old. Not so young. Good age for man.
No danger to the girl. No danger.

> *The* MOTHER, *who has been following this with
> increasing anxiety, suddenly leaps at* MADAME
> PACE, *her arms flailing.* MADAME PACE *catches
> her skilfully by the wrists, holds them, forcing the*
> MOTHER *to her knees, where she leaves her,
> turning to find a dominant position for herself
> upstage from where she coolly observes what
> follows.*

MOTHER You filthy — filthy — filthy —!
STEPDAUGHTER Oh, Mammy, don't, don't —
FATHER (*To* MOTHER) That's enough out of you now.
Go sit over there with the two children.
MOTHER Get her out of here! Get her out of here!
MADAME PACE No. I will go myself. When I decide to go. But
not before.
FATHER (*To* DIRECTOR) You see how it won't work this
way —
STEPDAUGHTER The two of them, you see —
FATHER In the one place at the one time, like — That's
why she didn't come with us in the first place.
DIRECTOR Don't worry. It's just a rough try-out. We'll get
something out of it. Start again, would you —
STEPDAUGHTER (*Runs wildly at* MADAME PACE) Start again! Tell
me again! What to do!
MADAME PACE No.
STEPDAUGHTER Tell me!
MADAME PACE No! Not with her (*Mother*) there.
STEPDAUGHTER Old man — ten minutes. Tell me! Quickly!
Now! We have to act it! Now!
MADAME PACE Tell her (*Mother*) to go away!
STEPDAUGHTER No, she has to be here. To find us. But first I
must do it. With him!
MADAME PACE I've played my part. Do it as you do it. I am
finished.

Exits.

STEPDAUGHTER Never mind her! She's gone! Gone!

DIRECTOR Gone? Gone where? Is she back there?

STEPDAUGHTER She's gone, gone! (*To* FATHER, *very rapidly*) Enter! Enter! No, don't bother going back out again — Just pretend you've walked in, see. Come here, over here, I'm waiting, I don't look up at you, go on, go on, say what you have to say, hello, miss, say it, you don't know me, you just see this piece of goods, waiting for you —

DIRECTOR Hey, hang on there. Who's directing this, you or me? Ha-ha. Well. (*To* FATHER) Oh, all right, do as she says. Just go upstage. Up to the door. Don't go out! Turn, good. Just as if you'd come in. Right. Now, come down again — (*To* ASM) Make sure you record all this, now. Thank you. Quiet, everyone!

> *Before they begin the* STEPDAUGHTER *rises, everyone watching, and goes and takes the hat from the rail, putting it on, slowly, almost reverently, before taking her seat.* FATHER *and* STEPDAUGHTER *now in character for the scene: he, partly excited, partly terrified at what he is doing; she, knowing and vicious, waiting to pounce.*

FATHER Hello, miss.

STEPDAUGHTER Hello.

FATHER It's not your — ah — It's not the first time for you, is it?

STEPDAUGHTER No.

FATHER That's fine so. That's grand. You're telling the truth now, aren't you?

STEPDAUGHTER Yes.

FATHER That's great so. It won't be too bad, will it? (*Tries to lift hat*) Here, let's have a look at you —

STEPDAUGHTER No, no!

> *She removes the hat herself. The* MOTHER, *who has been watching with increasing tension, now cries out to* DIRECTOR.

MOTHER Oh, please, sir, stop him, stop him —

> *The* FATHER *stands still, as if shocked by this. Pause. Then he slowly resumes.*

FATHER (*Taking hat*) Here, let me hang it up for you. (*He takes the hat and puts it back on the rail*) There's very nice clothes here. All kinds of nice clothes. Wouldn't you like to put some of them on? For me?

ACTRESS 1 Oh, my God, they're my things!

DIRECTOR Please! Just let them get on with it! No one is going to do anything to your — Keep going, keep going, please —

FATHER I like them — to dress up, girls. Girls like to dress up —

STEPDAUGHTER No.

FATHER (*Fury, out of nowhere*) You'll do as I say! Do you hear! Do everything! (*Shift*) Just don't make me cross. All right so. Madame Pace wouldn't like that, wouldn't like that at all. Making me cross. (*Takes out the envelope and puts it on the table*) There now. That's for you, now. Hmm?

STEPDAUGHTER Clothes! (*Holds out the sleeve of her coat with its mourning patch*) What does that mean on my clothes? The black diamond patch on my sleeve!

FATHER (*Confused, unsettled*) Someone's died. Someone's dead, is it?

ACTOR 2 What is it?

DIRECTOR She's wearing a black patch. They used to wear it as a sign of mourning. All right. (*To* ASM) Just cut that last bit off the tape. There's something

	— forced — about all this. Not quite right, somehow —
FATHER	(*Anguished*) But that is how it is!
DIRECTOR	Oh, don't get me wrong. It's great! It really is. We'll pick it up again now in a moment. (*Turns away to* ACTORS *as if the Family no longer exist*) Well? What do you think? That worked, didn't it? The clothes bit —
ACTRESS 1	When do I get my things back?
DIRECTOR	Not now! Not now, for heavensakes —
STEPDAUGHTER	(*Scream*) Why can't we go on?
DIRECTOR	All right! All right! Just take it easy for a minute, OK? God! (*To* ACTORS) Actually, the more I think about it, the more I think we should go for the grotesque humour of it —
ACTOR 1	But stylized, surely? I mean —
ACTRESS 1	It seems very straightforward to me. Very basic. I wouldn't clutter it up with all sorts of — you know?
DIRECTOR	No, but there is this weird sub-text to it, sort of macabre treatment of intimacy — know what I mean? — this stuff about clothes, costuming —
ACTRESS 1	Why don't we get into that later on?
DIRECTOR	Want to have a go?
ACTRESS 1	Sure.
DIRECTOR	Right away?
ACTOR 1	Absolutely! (*Leaps up, goes up to door*) 'Enter elderly gent!'
FATHER	(*Weakly, to* DIRECTOR, *who ignores him*) Mister —

The DIRECTOR *simply moves the* FATHER *and* STEPDAUGHTER *to one side.* ACTRESS 1 *has walked to clothes rail, examining the hat.*

DIRECTOR	What are you doing?
ACTRESS 1	Getting the hat.
DIRECTOR	Oh, all right so. Now! You've just had your encounter with this Madame Whatsit. What she has said to you has drained away any self-

respect you might have had. You feel *soiled*. *Abused*! You *want* to sell yourself. It wouldn't matter who or what walked in that door. You just sit here. Passive. The complete victim.

STEPDAUGHTER (*High pitched*) It's not like that!

DIRECTOR Silence, please!

STEPDAUGHTER She's not even dressed in mourning!

ACTRESS 1 All in good time. (*Loaded*) — Dear! (*To* DIRECTOR) Can we have less of the interruptions, please!

DIRECTOR (*To* STEPDAUGHTER) Look! It's your turn to watch now. OK? Let's go, let's go —

ACTOR 1 *prances through the door, the elderly rake on the prowl. Both he and the actress find a style that is far removed from the 'original': the rake and the inexperienced prostitute. The* ASM *acts as prompter.*

ACTOR 1 Hello, miss.

FATHER (*Unable to stop himself*) No-no, not like that at all — (*The* STEPDAUGHTER *gives a high-pitched screech of laughter*)

DIRECTOR Oh, my God, would you just keep out of this! And you (*Stepdaughter*)!

STEPDAUGHTER Sorry, can't help it, it's only, well, it's her (*Actress 1*)! Just sitting there, if that was me and he said Hello, miss, like that, I'd burst out laughing, I couldn't help it!

FATHER Exactly, mister, it's the way he says it, you see —

DIRECTOR 'The way he says it' — 'the way he says it!' — Look, just stay out of this, would you? Altogether! Right?

ACTOR 1 I see him as this old codger, bit of a lech, getting on, know what I mean?

DIRECTOR Just ignore them, would you! From the top, again — Well?

ACTOR 1 Very well. Ah — Hello, miss.

ACTRESS 1 Hello.

59

ACTOR 1 It's not the first time for you, I hope.

FATHER No-no, not 'I hope'. 'Is it?' he should say, 'is it?'. 'It's not the first time for you, is it?' Also, 'It's not — it's not', that should be said twice, not once —

ACTOR 1 I could swear he said 'hope'. (*To* ASM) What do you have there?

ASM I have 'is it'. 'It's not the first time for you, is it?'

ACTOR 1 Extraordinary — I could have sworn —

DIRECTOR 'Is it?' 'Hope', so what! Keep going, keep going, no, hang on a minute. One thing. (*To* ACTOR 1) Lighten it up, a bit, OK? A bit more — debonair — Let me show you the kind of thing I have in mind. (*Goes to door, turns, makes his entrance*) Hello, miss.

ACTRESS 1 Hello.

DIRECTOR Maybe not so furtive, not so shifty, you see. He's conscious of his own power, isn't he? The male thing. But a bit of style, a bit of dash. (*Lifts the hat*) 'And this isn't the first time you've been here, is it now?' etcetera etcetera. That kind of thing. OK?

ACTRESS 1 Shall I go on? (*Picking up*) No, sir.

ACTOR 1 So you've been here before, then. Many times?

FATHER But, mister —

DIRECTOR Hold it there! Give her time to get in the nod. Once. Twice. Like that. (*Actress 1*) Then she lifts her head. Slowly. Deep revulsion, now. That's it!

A screech of half-suppressed laughter from the STEPDAUGHTER. *All stare at her.*

STEPDAUGHTER Sorry — sorry — it's only —

DIRECTOR (*To* ACTORS) Go on —

ACTOR 1 Why don't you let me take your hat for you? And put it over here.

FATHER Mister!

The STEPDAUGHTER *explodes in laughter, savage, almost like tears.*

STEPDAUGHTER I can't — can't stop —

ACTRESS 1 That's it! I've had it! Letting that — creature — behave like that! It's — intolerable, that's what it is —

ACTOR 1 Me too. Let's just call the whole thing off!

DIRECTOR (*To* STEPDAUGHTER) You see what you've done!

STEPDAUGHTER It's all wrong!

FATHER Mister, mister, you must — forgive her. Forgive us all. We all feel the same. Seeing this. Us but not us, don't you know. Oh, they're lovely actors, lovely actors, but it's not us, mister, they're not us —

DIRECTOR Of course they're not you — That's the whole bloody point, isn't it? They're actors! Actors!

FATHER Actors, yes, course, acting. Oh, they're good, good, no mistake. It's only they want to *be* us, you see —

DIRECTOR And? Go on! Say what you have to say. Finish it —

FATHER Us and them —

DIRECTOR 'Us and them'? What's that supposed to mean?

FATHER It becomes theirs, you see. It's no longer ours —

DIRECTOR We've been through all this before —

FATHER Very peculiar to watch, very peculiar —

DIRECTOR (*To* ACTORS) This is worse than having a playwright present! My God! Look, the best thing is for us to do a read-through later on. On our own. OK? We'll have it all on tape. (*Back to* FATHER *and* STEPDAUGHTER) You two. Let's get back to your scene together and no giggling, mind!

STEPDAUGHTER There is no place for giggling anymore. From now on it's different —

DIRECTOR What? Oh, OK then. When you (*Father*) say 'someone's died'. Then you (*Stepdaughter*) say

'Forget it'. Then you (*Father*) answer 'I understand' and then you ask her —

STEPDAUGHTER (*Aggressively*) Yes! What did he ask?

DIRECTOR Let me see — he asks 'Who has died?' Yes — 'Who's dead? Who are you mourning?' Something like that.

STEPDAUGHTER No! He doesn't ask any such thing! He *tells* me to take off my frock. 'Why don't we take off your little frock? Hmm?' That's what he said!

DIRECTOR That's terrific! Terrific! That'll put them on the edge of their seats.

STEPDAUGHTER It's the truth!

DIRECTOR Oh, the truth — stop worrying about the truth!

STEPDAUGHTER And then? What then?

DIRECTOR Just leave it to me, OK?

STEPDAUGHTER No, I won't leave it to you! That's what you want, isn't it? To turn this disgusting moment into something entertaining. Something to move the crowd in the theatre. 'And why are you in mourning, dear?' 'Oh, sir, I'm in mourning because my Daddy died.' 'Oh, you poor thing, let me dry your eyes.' (*Loudly*) He must say what he said! He must do what he did! I must go behind that screen, shaking, my stomach retching, wondering if I'm going to — Pull off my dress, the rest of my things, stark naked, sick —

DIRECTOR No, no screen. We'll get rid of the screen altogether —

STEPDAUGHTER I want the truth to be told!

DIRECTOR But that is the truth! Out in the open, not hiding behind a bloody screen — (STEPDAUGHTER *starts to leave*) Hold it! Where are you going?

STEPDAUGHTER Leaving. I see what you're trying to do. You worked it out with him (*Father*), didn't you? He doesn't give a curse about how I feel, how I felt. All he's concerned about is getting to his big moment! His confession, his spiritual torment, his expiation, his forgiveness. I want my story told as it is!

DIRECTOR But, my dear! Everyone wants his story told as it is. The problem is to fit it in with everyone else's story. That's what theatre is about. Making every story fit with every other one. What we have to do in theatre is make the smallest moments tell the biggest stories. Sure, every character has his moment in the light. But it has to gel with the whole piece. Theatre may be a place of great egos, sure, but it's also the most democratic medium in existence. So, your story has to take its place, you know. And you must keep to your own place on the stage. Besides. This disgust that you talk about. You said yourself you had many men at the establishment of this Madame ah-Pace's. Not just him.

STEPDAUGHTER Every man I had was him.

DIRECTOR I beg your pardon!

STEPDAUGHTER They were all him! He is every man who ever used me! Because he made me the way I am.

DIRECTOR (*Low*) What a burden of guilt you lay on him and still you won't let him act it all out. Why are you doing this?

STEPDAUGHTER Very well. Let him act it out so! As long as you won't let him skip anything. As long as you won't let him avoid holding in his arms that child — 'Why don't we take your little frock off now?' That child, woman, child, standing watching her as she came out the school gate, stripping her with his eyes — (*The* FATHER *roars 'No!' and the* MOTHER *weeps*) Funny how no one knows our story now but tomorrow night your curtain will go up and you'll present our story, in your fashion, to the public — But they will never see the reality. Do you want to see the reality?

DIRECTOR Of course. That is why I allow you to be here in the first place.

STEPDAUGHTER	Well, then. Ask my mother to go outside.
MOTHER	For God's sake, no, sir! Please!
DIRECTOR	I'm sorry, but we have to see how it goes —
MOTHER	Don't let them, sir, oh, please don't let them!
DIRECTOR	But what's the problem? It's happened already, it's over and done with —
MOTHER	No, sir! It's happening now, now. It is always happening now! Over and over. (*Pointing*) Why are my children dumb? I ask you that question. They are dumb because they no longer exist. They're only here as a reminder, reminder. And she (*Stepdaughter*) is lost, gone, but why is she here now? A reminder, reminder of what I must suffer. All reminders. Over and over again.
FATHER	Eternal moment, mister, as I explained to you. Why is she (*Stepdaughter*) here? To fix me forever in that one eternal moment of my sin. She can't stop herself, you see. She has to go through with her role. And no changes you make can change that, can change my eternal torment, this eternal moment.
DIRECTOR	Yes. I can see all that. The whole thing builds up to the moment when she (*Mother*) catches you in the act, so to speak, right? Yes, that's how it goes, doesn't it?
FATHER	Her scream —
STEPDAUGHTER	It's ringing in my ears, that scream! (*Quickly*) Yes, play me whatever way you want, dressed, undressed, I don't care, do you hear? Don't care, only, my arm, you must have my arm — bare — like this — (*Rushes to* FATHER, *puts his arms around her, her head on his chest*) because when he — took — me, like this, I could see this vein in my arm, alive, the horror of it! Scream, Mammy, scream, damn you, scream, would you!

The MOTHER *screams and rushes between them,*

64

dragging away her daughter.

MOTHER You bastard! Don't you see who this is? It's my own child! The child of your own wife! Your own stepdaughter!

The DIRECTOR, *hands in the air, stops the action. The three figures sink away from one another as if wound down. Only the* FATHER *responds to the* DIRECTOR, *following in his steps. The* DIRECTOR *thinks a moment, his hands behind his head. He wheels about, nodding, very satisfied. He walks up and down, thinking things through, followed by the anxious* FATHER.

DIRECTOR Terrific! Thank you, everyone! That's it!

FATHER But, mister —

DIRECTOR One, the clinch. Two, her scream. She rushes over. Her line. Blackout. Great.

FATHER That's how it really happened, mister, really —

DIRECTOR We'll make that the end of Act One, shall we? (*Claps hands*) Bam! Blackout! Blackout! (*There is, indeed, an immediate blackout*) For Christsakes. I didn't mean a blackout now! You idiots! Get the bloody lights on again! Hey! (*Lights back on again. To* ASM, *who shrugs*) Who the hell is up in that lighting box? Never mind. (*To* FATHER) It works, though. Don't you think? She gives the line, rushes over to you two, ah-lights, and so on! (*To others*) Sorry about that cock-up, everyone. Let's get on with Act Two, shall we?

FATHER (*Real grief*) Everything is far too — quick!

STEPDAUGHTER (*Rushing forward*) We can't do the rest of it out here. By the fountain!

DIRECTOR And why not?

STEPDAUGHTER (*Pointing to* SON) Because of him!

DIRECTOR Who?

STEPDAUGHTER Him! Him! He's never out in the open air, he

spends his days cooped up in his room, drawing mad pictures on walls — And that child
there (*Little Boy*) — I told you what happens to
him inside the house —

DIRECTOR I know, I know — No problem. You can move
from place to place on stage without the
slightest difficulty. That's what's wonderful
about the stage, you know —

STEPDAUGHTER And do you put up signs saying where you're
at?

DIRECTOR Good God, no!

ACTRESS 2 That's old hat!

DIRECTOR The simpler the effect the better, audiences
are extremely sophisticated nowadays, you
know —

ACTOR 2 This isn't Brecht!

ACTOR 1 You see, theatre is based upon what the audience is made to believe —

ACTRESS 1 We make the audience believe —

ACTOR 1 Then everything, anything, becomes possible
on stage —

ACTRESS 1 A wonderful illusion, you see —

FATHER (*Cry*) Illusion! Illusion! Please, mister, don't let
them use that word. For us it is a terrible word,
a kind of curse.

DIRECTOR Illusion?

FATHER No — no — please —

DIRECTOR But we're only talking about staging something —

ACTRESS 1 — it's our art —

FATHER Course! Course! Forgive me. I know the way
you feel — here — in this place — it all seems
— like a game, maybe —

ACTOR 1 Game! This isn't a game!

ACTRESS 1 We are serious artists.

FATHER Course you are, course you are and then you
create this illusion of what is real —

DIRECTOR So? So?

FATHER But, you see, for us, us six, we have no existence outside illusion. That is our reality, full stop. Know what I mean, mister?

DIRECTOR Yes — yes — no, I don't, actually —

FATHER (*Smile*) You play. We live. What you play at, here in this place, we *live*. And it's our only life. Half-finished. But fixed. Never to change. Do you know what that means? It means we know exactly who we are. (*To* DIRECTOR) Do you know who you are, mister?

DIRECTOR Oh, come on —

FATHER But, no, suppose I were to tell you that you were me, what would you say, now?

DIRECTOR I'd say you were nuts. (ACTOR *laughter*)

FATHER Would you now? And it's a big joke, is it? And this gentleman here (*Actor 1*), he is me, is he? When he's clearly himself. And I'm clearly myself and that's a joke too, is it? Hmm?

DIRECTOR Look, could we just cut out the chat and get on with it —

FATHER But what I'm asking is that we drop the joke and stop the play-acting and I ask you, again, mister: Who are you?

DIRECTOR (*Uncomfortable with this. To* ACTORS) Have you ever heard the like?

FATHER (*Dreamily*) A character can always ask a man who he is. You see, a character is always — someone. Never anyone else. Always fixed. Whereas a man can be many things. And sometimes may even be nothing at all —

DIRECTOR Well, I'm someone, I can assure you —

FATHER Of course you say that —

DIRECTOR That's it, then — ?

FATHER Do you remember how it was, when you were young, how you dreamed? They were illusions, and no mistake! Dreams! Never to come true. All gone. Doesn't it make you realize that today is only an illusion, too, and also tomorrow, that these boards you stand on, the very ground below them, is all illusion? Hmm?

DIRECTOR I've had enough of this. It's getting us nowhere.

FATHER Nowhere is right. It's only to show the way
people live, the way what seems real one day
is gone up in smoke the next. That's not the
way we are, mister.

DIRECTOR I see. So what you've been putting on for us is
more real that what we do, is that it?

FATHER That's it —

DIRECTOR Is it so?

FATHER I thought you saw that right away, mister.

DIRECTOR And you're telling me that you're more real
than I am?

FATHER No doubt about it. You see, you change, I
don't.

DIRECTOR Everyone and everything on earth changes,
for God's sake!

FATHER (*Cry: part anguish, part frustration*) We do not
change, we never change, can never change,
and that is our — curse! Fixed for all time.
Don't you feel this — coldness, mister, when
you are near us?

DIRECTOR (*Lost*) I've never imagined this kind of thing
about characters before —

FATHER That's because authors hide their tricks. They
pretend that characters are flesh and blood.
And people believe them. Haven't you wondered sometimes what a character was doing
while off the stage? Have you sometimes wondered what a character did before the story
began or after it ended? You needn't wonder.
Outside the prison of the story there is a noth-
ingness. Beyond the stage there is only silence
and nothing.

DIRECTOR Oh, all that's rather obvious, isn't it? I mean —

FATHER Then the horror of being invented by an author
who never finishes what was begun. Imagine
that! Do you blame us for coming here, as we
do? In search of an author? Alive but with no

life. How we haunted his study, now one of us, now another, then all six of us, whispering in his ear —

DIRECTOR Who? Whose ear?

FATHER Pirandello's!

STEPDAUGHTER (*On cue, exact tone of the Father*) He would sit there, in the dusk, an old man dreaming of a young love, sunk in an armchair, too tired to get up and light the lamp, and as the darkness gathered we would come and stand around him, whispering our hopes to him, tempting him with our futures, futures that would never be, our untold stories that would never be told to the end, my mother, the two children. Him (*the Son*) always hanging back. Him (*the Father*) and me. Then me alone, tempting him —

FATHER (*Peevish*) You probably did more damage than good! You probably put him off altogether, oh yes, you — the strap!

STEPDAUGHTER (*Ignoring him; to* DIRECTOR) But *you'll* hear our story, won't you?

DIRECTOR At this stage it might be a relief — All right, some action, please — (*To* STEPDAUGHTER) Now. You told me about him (*Son*) locked into his room; the little boy there, wandering the house, hiding behind doors, thinking up his terrible plan —

STEPDAUGHTER And her (*Little Girl*), the little one —

DIRECTOR Yes, the little girl out in the garden, playing by herself. That's the way you have it, isn't it? The little boy in the house, the little girl out by the fountain?

STEPDAUGHTER In the sunshine — a child playing — a garden, then a bedroom, a bed, she sleeps, beside me, my corrupt body, her innocence, holding me with her little arms, my body — (*Distraught*) that garden, that fountain, she picks the flowers —

DIRECTOR It's OK. No problem. We'll fit the whole thing into the garden. You'll see. (*To* ASM) Let's get those trees in. (*To* STEPDAUGHTER) The little boy doesn't have to do his hiding in the house, see. He can hide behind trees in the garden. What about that?

ASM (*Calling off*) Let's have those trees in, please! Over here. Thank you.

Trees are flown into the garden area.

DIRECTOR Could do with a backdrop, too. Behind that fountain. (*A white sheet is dropped down*) That all you got? Oh, forget it, it's OK. Let's light that, then. (*Moonlight effect*) How about that? He (*Little Boy*) doesn't have to be indoors at all, see. He can do his hiding out here, behind those trees. Now, young man, it's your go. Over here, please! Hey! Wake up! What's up with him? Can't anyone get him to talk? OK, no talk, fine. (*Grabs the* LITTLE BOY *and pushes him*) Just get over there, behind these trees. Hide, hide-and-seek, right? Peep out. Ah, that's it, good man! Maybe if we were to get the little girl to run over and whisper to him? He might say something? No?

STEPDAUGHTER Not a hope. He won't talk. Not as long as he's (*Son*) around.

DIRECTOR What's he got to do with it?

STEPDAUGHTER First you have to get rid of him! (*Pointing to* SON)

SON (*Getting ready to leave*) Suits me fine.

DIRECTOR No! Don't go! Stay right where you are!

The only other one who reacts strongly to all this is the MOTHER who throws her hands up as if to stop the SON.

SON Never wanted to be here in the first place. I

don't belong here —

DIRECTOR What do you mean? You're family, aren't you?

SON Family! (*As the* DIRECTOR *grabs him*) Leave me alone, will you! I'm going!

STEPDAUGHTER (*Taunting*) Let him go! He won't get far.

FATHER There has to be that terrible scene! Between him and his mother!

SON There has to be nothing!

He breaks free and when the DIRECTOR *tries again to stop him the* STEPDAUGHTER *comes and releases the* SON *from the* DIRECTOR. *All watch as the* SON *makes a series of bizarre, half-running attempts to 'escape'. It's as if he runs into blank walls around the stage. He ends up weeping in frustration.*

STEPDAUGHTER Watch this, now! All of ye! (*To* SON) Go on! Go! Run! (*Screech of laughter*) Can't — can't — can't — See that! He's stuck with us, family — family — family — Can't leave Daddy, can't leave Mammy — stuck! Only I can escape. Only me. I'm the only one able. When it's all over. But he's left. With Mammy and Daddy. Three of them. Three left out of six! (*Grabs* MOTHER *and steers her forward*) You want to, Mammy, don't you? You do. You want to act your terrible scene with him. Go on, go on, now!

The MOTHER *approaches the* SON, *her arms outstretched.*

SON Get away from me! I'm not acting anything!

FATHER (*To* DIRECTOR) Make him act, mister!

SON No one can make me!

FATHER By Christ, I'll make you!

SON Take your hands off me!

STEPDAUGHTER Stop! Both of you! First off, there's my little sister there. (*Takes the* LITTLE GIRL *to her*) Oh, you look so lost! Don't you know where you are? You're on a stage. Where people dress up and — play. Make-believe, but real, too. Oh, my poor darling, what an awful part has been given to you to play! Here! This is the garden, there's the pool. Of course it's all pretend, isn't it? Pretend for everyone here. Except for you. Because you're playing in real life, real pool, real water, real lily pads and, over there, real little ducks. No, your mother isn't paying the slightest attention. She's too wrapped up in that room with him! (*Son*) But I'm here! I'm always here because I am possessed, you see, possessed! And as for him! (*Little Boy*)

She suddenly abandons the LITTLE GIRL *and runs to the* LITTLE BOY, *grabbing him forcefully.*

Why didn't you see her drown? Why? What're you up to? Out with it! What's in your pocket? (*She pulls his hand out: he's holding a gun*)

DIRECTOR Is that a prop?

STEPDAUGHTER Where did you get that? Answer! Useless. You little fool, you! You shouldn't be shooting yourself, you know. You should shoot one of them! Him! (*Father*) Or him! (*Son*) That's what I would do. If I were you. But I'm not, am I? Go on! Hide!

She moves him behind one of the trees. She walks slowly to the LITTLE GIRL, *lifts her ceremoniously in her arms and carries her to the pool. She lays her down within, arranging her, face down, with great solemnity.*

DIRECTOR Very nice, keep it going. (*To* SON) While this was going on, you were —

SON 'While this was going on' — nothing! Nothing! Ask her! (*Mother*)

The MOTHER *does indeed step forward so that she, the* SON *and* DIRECTOR *engage one another. At the same time* ACTOR 2 *and* ACTRESS 2 *come up behind the* SON *and* MOTHER, *the better to observe them in action.*

MOTHER That's the truth, sir. I walked into his room —

SON My room! Room! Get it? Not garden, room!

DIRECTOR Don't worry about that. We can set anything anywhere on stage —

SON (*To* ACTOR 2) What the hell are you up to?

ACTOR 2 Nothing. Just carry on. I'm just — watching — that's all —

SON (*To* ACTRESS 2) And I suppose you're just — watching — her (*Mother*)? To learn how to act?

DIRECTOR Relax, would you — they're simply researching their parts, that's all. For later on.

SON Thank you very much. Their parts! You're wasting your bloody time, you know that? All you'll ever do is skim the surface, my friends. And you know what it's like for us? Watching you — act! Huh! It's like looking at this — this — into a cracked mirror. Whose arm is this? Whose head is that? Bits of us here! Bits of us there! No one whole. No one — finished.

FATHER (*Loud cry of grief*) The boy is speaking the truth. All of you. Attend to him, now —

DIRECTOR (*To* ACTORS) OK, just leave it for the present.

They step aside.

SON I'm not even — present — here —

DIRECTOR Just be quiet. I want to hear your mother. (*To* MOTHER) You went into his room —?

MOTHER Into his room I went. I couldn't stand it anymore, you see, sir. I had to pour out what was inside me —

SON But I wouldn't stay. I ran out. I hate people who make scenes —

MOTHER   What he says is true, sir. He never liked scenes of any kind —

DIRECTOR   I see. Well, this is one scene we've got to have, what happened between the two of you —

SON   — no scene, was no scene —

MOTHER   I'd be glad to do it, sir, but first I'd have to have a minute alone with him. To talk to him, first, in private, like — so much to say —

FATHER   (*To* SON) Speak to your own mother, dammit —

SON   No! I'm saying nothing!

FATHER   As God is my judge, I'll make you —

He and the SON *wrestle about to general consternation.*

SON   Leave me alone, you clown!

FATHER   Clown! Clown, is it? Your own mother, your mother —

MOTHER   Stop them, oh, stop them, someone!

The SON *throws the* FATHER *who actually falls. Everyone is shocked into silence by what has happened.*

DIRECTOR   Right, everybody, could we all calm down please —

SON   That's the horror! Everything so — public! If it isn't one of you it's another of you, parading our disgrace in front of everyone. I hate it! I hate the way you expose yourselves, hate it, hate it, hate it — I want no part of it. Ever!

DIRECTOR   But you came here. To this theatre — like the rest of them —

SON   I was dragged here, dragged here. Because he (*Father*) was determined and she (*Stepdaughter*) was determined to play it out —

DIRECTOR   Yes, but play out what?

SON   Not only what really happened. But also what had yet to be imagined —

DIRECTOR OK, look, just let's keep to the story, the basic story, forget everything else. Back to the situation, OK? You left the room without saying a word?

SON Yes.

DIRECTOR And? Go on, go on —

SON (*Begins to move, shuffling, in a daze*) Cross the garden —

He stops dead.

DIRECTOR Yes! Go on! Cross the garden —

SON I can't go on —

DIRECTOR You must go on!

SON — her —

DIRECTOR Who? Her? (*Points to* STEPDAUGHTER, SON *shakes his head. The* MOTHER *starts to weep loudly and she points toward the fountain*) The little girl, isn't it? (*All look to the fountain, except the* SON *who stares straight out*)

SON (*His back to the others*) In the fountain —

DIRECTOR What did you do then?

SON (*Slowly, working it out*) I think I may have lost my mind. Of course I rushed over there. The fountain. I could see everything. But first I couldn't — *think*. She was floating head down, dress wet, one hand sticking out. Like this. I could hear myself, saying to myself, like a stranger: Lift her out of there, for fuck sake! But I didn't, you see. Next I looked over to the side. Behind those bushes over there. The kid was standing there with a gun in his hand. He was still a child but his face was the face of an old man. Then he shot himself.

A sudden report of a single gunshot from behind the trees.

MOTHER (*Loud scream*) My little boy! Oh, my little boy!

She rushes behind the trees, followed by everyone except the FATHER *(centre thrust stage) and the* DIRECTOR *(downstage), both with bowed heads. Murmuring, weeping from behind the trees. The* DIRECTOR *then looks at the* FATHER *who shrugs, once. They stare at one another throughout what follows. A beat. Then uproar, people giving different directions, loud wails of grief from* MOTHER *and* STEPDAUGHTER. *Then, quickly, the bloodied figure of the* LITTLE BOY *is carried on and then off again behind the back screen, a sort of confused procession.*

DIRECTOR   He's not hurt, is he? (*Confused*) Hope he hasn't hurt himself. Sometimes happens — on stage.

He looks at the FATHER *who shrugs again. We now see the* DIRECTOR *full-face: he is trying to work out what has happened. The rest of the acting company drift back on again. First* ACTRESS 1, *very distraught, supported by* ACTOR 1 *and* ASM. *Then, behind them,* ACTRESS 2, *dark and disturbed. Finally,* ACTOR 2, *excited, jumpy.*

ACTRESS 1   (*Tears*) Oh, he's dead, he's dead, poor little boy! What a dreadful thing to happen!
   ACTOR 1   (*Hearty laugh*) Oh, you dear, silly girl! It's nothing. Just a performance. And what a performance!
ACTRESS 1   No — no — no —
        ASM   He's all right, dear. He really is.
ACTRESS 2   (*High, almost hysterical*) Why have we each seen different things?
   ACTOR 2   It's like — you know? — the ultimate joke. Only nobody laughs.
     FATHER   (*Great roar which stops everyone in his tracks*) Joke? Joke, is it? Ladies and Gentlemen! This is no joke! This is the real thing!

He turns on his heel and makes a slow exit, watched by all the others. The rest of the company turns and looks to the DIRECTOR, *appealing. Lost within himself, he now has to shake himself, gathering his things together.*

DIRECTOR Thanks. That's it, everybody.

ACTRESS 2 Are we finished?

ACTOR 2 We can't be! We have to pick it all up now. Go with it!

ACTRESS 1 (*To* ACTOR 1) Did you see his face? The little boy?

DIRECTOR (*To* ACTRESS 1) You're too hard on yourself, you know. You mustn't put yourself through hell all the time. Just remember: It had nothing to do with you. Nothing!

ACTRESS 1 But we saw it! We *all* saw it!

ACTOR 1 (*To* DIRECTOR) Couldn't agree more with you! This had nothing to do with what we do. Nothing!

ACTOR 2 That's because you close yourself off!

DIRECTOR (*Very strongly, to* ACTOR 2) Yeah, and that's the only way to get work done on stage. Knowing *when* to close yourself off. Otherwise all you're doing is turning on and off emotions. Like a bloody tap. Useless.

ACTRESS 2 (*To* ACTOR 2) Hey! Take it easy.

DIRECTOR OK. Let's just leave it at that. We tried. We did our best. You all know that. Somehow, in the end, we couldn't — (*Searching for the word*) connect with those — (*Gestures off*) Somehow we were always only their — (*Ironically*) audience.

ACTOR 1 That it, then?

DIRECTOR Yep.

ACTOR 1 Are we continuing tomorrow? With the same scene?

DIRECTOR Sure. Why not? Let's just see what we can make of it now. After all — (*Gestures*) — this —

77

ACTRESS 1 I simply cannot close off what I experience. I can't. Ever.

DIRECTOR Look. Stop worrying. You're going to be OK.

As they all begin to gather their things they are stopped by a shrill scream of laughter from the STEPDAUGHTER, *off. All freeze. Hold this. It is as if each one is lost in a separate memory.*

The back screen lights up. Moving/slide images of the STEPDAUGHTER *on the same road as before. She is running away from us, looking back, while all the time she gives out this hysterical laughter, which dies as she disappears into the distance. As the screen goes blank everyone on stage bustles about, gathering up scripts and belongings.*

ASM (*To* DIRECTOR) Same time tomorrow?

DIRECTOR (*He is leaving*) Right! Same time, same place. Bye, everybody —

ASM Same time, same place tomorrow, everybody!

She leaves. ACTOR 1 *and* ACTRESS 1 *leave together.*

ACTOR 1 (*As he goes*) Do you know? In that scene. Somehow I still don't know these people. Know what I mean — ?

ACTRESS 1 (*As she goes*) That poor child! Those poor children!

They are quickly followed by ACTOR 2 *and* ACTRESS 2, *talking as they go.*

ACTOR 2 You know something? I've been thinking. Maybe it's the only way for theatre to go from now on? Get it straight off the streets. Just open the doors! Let it all pour in. Anyone and everyone!

ACTRESS 2 That's not what it's about. What about the role

of the writer? And the director?

ACTOR 2 Who needs a director? Who needs a writer?

ACTRESS 2 Oh, really? You mean: Why Pirandello?

> *As they leave, lights down on the stage. The front screen is dropped in. It lights up and we see the* FATHER, *the* MOTHER *and the* SON *(still to one side, lagging behind) as they walk tiredly away from us into the distance, into Nowhere. On this image all the lights come down and the play ends.*

HENRY

after HENRY IV

Characters

HENRY, *a former film star and now the mad king*

The Four Young Actors
   LANDOLF (BOBBY)
   HAROLD (NICK)
   ORDULF (JOCK)
   BERTOLD (JOE)

The Five Visitors
   MARGARET, *Henry's former lover*
   FRIEDA, *her daughter*
   THOMAS, *Margaret's current lover*
   CARL, *Henry's nephew*
   THE DOCTOR, *an experimental therapist*

Time and Place

The present. A remote house, a house of images, maintained as a retreat, an asylum, for Henry.

Henry was commissioned by Pittsburgh Irish and Classical Theatre (PICT), Inc, and first presented at the Charity Randall Theatre in Pittsburgh, Pennsylvania, on September 3, 2005, with the following cast:

HENRY	Richard McMillan
LANDOLF	Joe Schulz
ORDULPH	Martin Giles
HAROLD	Patrick Jordan
BERTOLD	Ben Hersey
CARL	Joel Ripka
FRIEDA	Erin Keom
MARGARET	Robin Walsh
DOCTOR	Larry John Meyers
THOMAS	Sam Tsoutsouvas

Direction	Andrew S. Paul
Set design	Frank Conway
Costume design	Cletus Anderson
Lighting design	Cindy Limauro
Sound design	Elizabeth Atkinson
Video design	Ciara Moore and Buzz Miller

ACT ONE

Piercing sound/music throughout the opening.

The space is dominated by large, distorting mirrors facing audience and a magnificent, elaborate throne on a dais. On the throne is a splendid gold crown.

Enter BERTOLD, *casual contemporary clothes, a bag slung over one shoulder, examining this strange environment, half intrigued, half scared. He starts suddenly and tries to hide as* HENRY *enters in a stylish business suit, the only thing about him that is normal. For instance, his make-up is garish. He wears a paper crown, a party hat, the kind that comes from a Christmas cracker or children's party.* BERTOLD *becomes a second 'audience' of what follows, watching* HENRY *from a hiding place.*

HENRY *stands before the mirrors, back to audience, and examines his face, eyes, nose, and neck, a distraught, anguished figure. Multiple images in the mirrors. He turns slowly, comes forward and peers into the audience, a prisoner looking for escape. Behind him, the mirrors become giant video screens.* BERTOLD *doesn't see the screens; his eyes are only on* HENRY.

On the screens appears Henry's memory: a cavalcade of heavily costumed horsemen, larger than life-size, led by the crowned figures of the younger Henry and Margaret, playing the parts of Emperor Henry IV and the Marchesa of Tuscany. The effect is of a dark, brutal, stylized group galloping toward us (like a group of Kurosawa warriors). HENRY *is gripped by this apparition behind him, as if knowing what is to come.*

The sound/music rises to a high pitch and suddenly, on screen, Henry's horse rears, Henry is thrown, and the screens go blank. HENRY *reacts as if he has been thrown, falling forward onto the stage, losing his paper crown. His hair is streaked with dye.*

BERTOLD *examines the throne and crown while* HENRY *is still prostrate.* HENRY *staggers to his feet and* BERTOLD *hides behind the throne.* HENRY *walks back, goes and lifts the crown, turns to audience and crowns himself. The effect is transformative. Trumpets! Suddenly, he is truly a king as* BERTOLD *peeps at him in amazement.*

BERTOLD *jumps once more as* ORDULF *appears carrying penitential robes.* ORDULF *is in full period costume as an eleventh-century courtier.* BERTOLD *watches, transfixed, as* HENRY *gravely nods to* ORDULF. ORDULF *gently removes* HENRY's *crown.* HENRY *bows as* ORDULF *drapes a penitential robe over his shoulders.* HENRY *sinks to his knees.* ORDULF *scatters ashes over his head.*

Very rapid, halfhearted performance now follows of the scene at Canossa with HENRY *as Henry IV, prostrate in the snow before his enemies, Pope Gregory and the Marchesa of Tuscany, who look down at him from a lighted window: first,* LANDOLF *and* HAROLD *on, black T-shirts and jeans, pulling on costumes,* LANDOLF *as the Marchesa,* HAROLD *as Pope Gregory.* ORDULF *pushes the throne to one side and then helps* LANDOLF *to set up a 'window' above the kneeling* HENRY. HAROLD *spots the gaping* BERTOLD *and quickly pulls him off stage, still carrying his bag, rapidly bringing him back on again, without the shoulder bag but now pulling on makeshift period court costuming, perhaps just a cloak and hat.* BERTOLD *is signalled to stand and be quiet, which he does.*

HAROLD *and* LANDOLF, *with suitable, haughty, papal and aristocratic poses, take their places in the 'window' looking down on* HENRY, *still on his knees. Lighting on* HENRY *and the figures in the 'window'.* ORDULF *produces a CD player and we hear monks chanting the* Dies Irae, *together with mounting storm effects.* HENRY *throws up his arms before the figures in the 'window', grovels on his knees, hands up again, several times. Then, very quickly, the whole scene is struck once more.* ORDULF *hurries* HENRY *off. The 'window' is dismantled,* LANDOLF *and* HAROLD *remove their costumes. Heavy breathing after a 'good' performance!* BERTOLD *stands there, mouth open.*

BERTOLD   What the fuck was that all about?
LANDOLF   You can get your gear off now, sugar pie! Time out!
HAROLD   You're the new guy, right?

ORDULF *comes back on, removing his costume.*

ORDULF   OK, folks. He's back in his room. He's quiet.

BERTOLD (*Pointing off*) That's him, right? That old film star guy who's crazy? Thinks he's a king or something, right? Jeez, I don't know where I am!

HAROLD You're an actor as well, aren't you? You'll get used to it.

ORDULF You'll be OK, brother. Just go with it.

LANDOLF (*Speech*) We are all four of us actors, dear heart — playing our roles, our daily performance, with our mad star out there, our Henry.

HAROLD *And* we're well paid for it. Beats sitting around waiting for a call from the lousy agent.

BERTOLD But, just now? What were you all doing with him? All that stuff, bowing and so forth. (*To* LANDOLF) Drag, right?

LANDOLF (*Pose*) Pretty, no?

HAROLD Ever hear of Canossa?

BERTOLD Canossa, Canossa, yeah, that's the game that Jewish ladies play, right?

> General hilarity at this. 'Not a card game, darling!'
> 'Hey! He thinks he's in Miami!' 'Maybe the Catskills!'
> 'Card game! Wow!'

HAROLD It's a place, bud. Canossa. Italy. History, man!

> As LANDOLF speaks, a shutter opens high above the
> throne, not seen by the others, and HENRY appears
> there. He wears his tattered cloak and crown, observ-
> ing all below him but without the slightest reaction,
> a voyeur with his own secret observation point, an
> audience of what is happening below him.

LANDOLF (*Totally gripped by the image he is creating*) Just imagine! Canossa! An emperor, a king! For three whole days forced to kneel in the snow before the lighted window. And in the window, Pope Gregory, watching — and beside him the grand Marchesa of Tuscany, both of them — deadly enemies of the emperor! That's the Canossa scene. Awesome!

Above them HENRY *half cries out, the shutter closes, and he disappears from view.*

BERTOLD   Hey! — What's that?

HAROLD   (*To* ORDULF) You sure he's locked in that goddamn room of his?

ORDULF   Sure I'm sure.

BERTOLD   Is he — y'know? Dangerous?

HAROLD   Dangerous? Henry? Naw! Like a lamb, old Henry. Just so long as he gets his daily fix — in the snow — on his knees before the Pope. With that woman, in the window —

BERTOLD   Snow? Ya mean we're gonna get snow effects? Neat!

ORDULF   (*Grimly*) The snow is in Henry's mind.

BERTOLD   You mean you guys gotta do this Canossa stuff every day?

LANDOLF   *We* do it, dearie — (*Taps him on shoulder*) You're part of the team now, love!

BERTOLD   (*Looking around*) How the hell can he afford all this? It goes on all the time, right? Must cost a damn fortune to keep this caper going —

ORDULF   He was one of the richest guys in Hollywood. In his day, that is —

LANDOLF   He had this sister, see. She managed his money —

HAROLD   Multi-millionaires —

LANDOLF   Seen any of his movies?

BERTOLD   Naw. Never watch old movies —

LANDOLF   Love scenes — I will never forget his love scenes — (*Fake fainting fit*) Give me air, Mary! Wot a bodee!

BERTOLD   OK, OK. I get it — big deal — but now he spends all his loot on this — game? Can't believe it.

LANDOLF   Game? Did you say game? Not a game to him, dear boy. Not to our Henry. Oh, no. Absolutely not. To him this is — how shall I put it? — reality. Much more. To Henry this is the ultimate reality —

BERTOLD   He thinks he's this king character. That it?

ORDULF   Yep. Henry IV. And we play his courtiers. Easy-peasy.

LANDOLF Not *thinks*, darling. Wrong word again. He *knows* he's the king. *Knows*. And we're not exactly courtiers either. More like dashing young men about the court. Lovely idea that, actually, don't you think? Dashing young men —

BERTOLD And what about all this dumb history crap?

HAROLD That's the funny thing, actually. Of course, you need to know something. But Henry carries all the history around with him, in his head —

ORDULF All ya gotta do is follow what he does.

HAROLD — almost like he's directing —

ORDULF — that's it!

BERTOLD (*Demented*) That's it? Christ!

ORDULF To be honest, it's the easiest gig I've ever done —

HAROLD (*Bows to throne*) His Majesty, Henry IV!

BERTOLD Hey, that's another thing — which Henry IV are we talking about? Only Henry IV I know is Shakespeare —

The other three laugh heartily at this. 'Shakespeare!' 'Are you kidding?' 'Where's old Falstaff?'

LANDOLF This isn't Shakespeare, love. This is Pirandello!

HAROLD You mean to say — they didn't give you any research? Before coming here?

BERTOLD No-o.

LANDOLF Oh dear, I can see I'm going to have to start from first base with you, you poor thing!

BERTOLD Look! I just got this call yesterday from the agent. Given this address, remote house in the hills, they said, hard to find. It sure was — hard to find, I mean — don't know where I am at this stage —

LANDOLF (*Takes it all in*) Our house of illusion!

BERTOLD Young guy — called Carl — he interviewed me.

HAROLD That would be Henry's nephew.

BERTOLD King Henry's nephew? Young Carl?

HAROLD No-no-no, the *real* Henry's *real* nephew.

BERTOLD Can this get any worse?

HAROLD   You see Carl handles everything now since his mom died. All Henry's finances. This place — sort of — stage manager, you might say, young Carl — Yep! Like theatre — never thought of it like that before —

LANDOLF   But it was Carl's mother who set this place up. Henry's sister. She thought: Why not! He's never going to be cured. Let's get him out of that hospital. Let him play out his mad role — to the end of his life — So, now, Carl —

ORDULF   — he's the guy who delivers us the scratch, see —

BERTOLD   So? What gives? I get to be someone, right?

LANDOLF   You're Bertold!

BERTOLD   Bertold! Who the hell is Bertold?

LANDOLF   Haven't a clue, actually.

HAROLD   Just a few days ago Henry started yelling — no warning or anything, just yelling, 'Bring me Bertold! Bring me Bertold!'

LANDOLF   — so, here you are, darling — Bertold!

ORDULF   Oh, give the guy a break, would you — he can't take it all in —

LANDOLF   My dear boy, if it's any consolation to you we don't know who we are either. Oh, Henry has given us these names, sure. He's Harold, that's Ordulf, I'm Landolf. Names. Just names. But we haven't a clue who these people might be —

ORDULF   Just think of it as improv, like —

HAROLD   Personally, I hate improv. I build from inside — know what I mean?

LANDOLF   (*Actorly speech*) Names! Do we actors not live through names? He's right! (*Harold*) Not any different to the theatre, is it? You lose your own name. Take another one. Then stand around. Just to — attend on Henry —

ORDULF   We do whatever he says we should do — (*Realization*) Ya know something? I guess I'd do anything for that old guy — anything —

LANDOLF   — bit like — puppets, actually — waiting for someone to pull the strings —

BERTOLD I think I'm going to go nuts.

LANDOLF Oh, no. You're not nuts. (*Pointing off*) He's the one who is — as you put it so delightfully — nuts.

BERTOLD What happened to him? I mean he wasn't always like this, was he?

The other three look at one another: Who is going to explain?

HAROLD No-o.

BERTOLD Well?

ORDULF He fell off a horse.

BERTOLD Fell off a horse! Come on! That doesn't make you go bananas.

HAROLD One day he and his lady friend, woman called Margaret —

ORDULF — a whole bunch of people — dressed up in costume —

LANDOLF — twenty years ago —

HAROLD — sort of — cavalcade — out riding. Henry dressed up as the Holy Roman Emperor Henry IV, his chick, this Margaret dame, dressed up as his deadly enemy, the Marchesa of Tuscany —

LANDOLF That's right, the beautiful lady in the window at Canossa, played by me just now —

BERTOLD Just a mo! You mean his girlfriend was dressed up as his deadly enemy, I mean, Henry's — aw, for fuck sake, I can't follow this —

HAROLD — riding along beside one another — then it happened —

LANDOLF (*Gripped*) He was thrown violently to the ground. When he came to, he was, indeed, and for all time, Henry IV, Holy Roman Emperor —

HENRY *screams, off, and everyone freezes.* BERTOLD *is petrified, the others indifferent.*

HAROLD 't's OK. He yells like that — sometimes —

ORDULF — sometimes — I think he hears every damned

	thing we say — down here — know what I mean?
BERTOLD	How do you guys stay sane?
LANDOLF	(*Lost in thought*) Bad enough being an actor. But being an actor with such wealth. Must make the fantasy life mega! Not like us, you know, the extremely rich. For one thing, they can never be quite sure that they're living in the real world. And when you're an actor as well, what hope is there? Reality becomes extremely elusive. So! Henry likes to play the king.

> CARL *comes in, dressed in casual contemporary clothes. A moment to register his arrival.*

BERTOLD	Hey — look! It's that young guy, Carl, the one who gave me this part — (*To* CARL) Hi there!
ORDULF	Maybe it's payday!
CARL	(*To* BERTOLD) You're the new one, aren't you? Have you found your place?
BERTOLD	Found my place! Ha-ha-ha. Oh, boy! We're in a comedy, right?
LANDOLF	(*To* CARL) You're not usually here at this time —
HAROLD	Yeah — what gives?
CARL	There's to be an — examination —
BERTOLD	A what?
CARL	Nothing to do with you four — I've brought some visitors. For Henry.
ORDULF	Visitors? Any young chicks?
LANDOLF	(*Disgusted look at* ORDULF. *To* CARL) And may we at least ask? Who are these visitors?
CARL	Well, there's Margaret and her daughter Frieda —
LANDOLF	Margaret? You mean she's here!
BERTOLD	Hey, that's the dame in the window, right? I mean the dame on the horse — I mean the old guy's chick, right? Who was his deadly enemy — Jeez!
LANDOLF	She has never come here before — not in my time —
HAROLD	Wait! Who else is there?
CARL	It's really none of your concern —

LANDOLF But we should know —

CARL Very well. A gentleman. A friend of the women.
Also a doctor —

BERTOLD Doctor?

LANDOLF What kind of a doctor?

CARL That's quite enough, thank you. All of you, off,
now — come on — come on —

He gestures and HAROLD, ORDULF, LANDOLF *and*
BERTOLD *drift off around the back of the throne.*

LANDOLF (*Going*) A doctor, this might lead to something
interesting, indeed —

BERTOLD Are they going to be, ya know, performing as well,
these new guys? Know what I mean — costumes
and all?

CARL *checks out the place. As he does so* HENRY
appears high above the stage, a revengeful Prospero.
CARL *calls off in the direction from which he has
come.*

CARL You can all come in now. It's quite safe. He's
locked away.

Above him, HENRY *clicks his fingers, and the screens
glow with light.* MARGARET, *with* FRIEDA *on her
arm, leads on* THOMAS *and the* DOCTOR. *They are
all dressed in smart contemporary clothes.* THOMAS
carries the same dress worn by MARGARET, *all those
years ago, in the riding accident with* HENRY. *The
group freezes, clearly uncertain, even fearful, with*
CARL *watching them.* HENRY *clicks his fingers, with
each click a still of the riding cavalcade of twenty
years before, led by Henry and Margaret as Emperor
and Marchesa, flashes up on the screen. Then* HENRY
clicks his fingers, the screens turn blank. HENRY
*looks down, once, then disappears from view. The
group now breaks up:* THOMAS *and the* DOCTOR

examining the dress between them. MARGARET
*walks to one side, takes out some photographs and
looks at them.* FRIEDA *rushes over to* CARL.

FRIEDA Carl! I gotta get out of here. I'm scared!

CARL (*Embraces her*) This won't take long — Promise!

FRIEDA That man — your uncle — where is he?

CARL He's in his room. Look, there's nothing to worry
about.

FRIEDA This place is spooky — (*Urgently*) Got to talk to
you — Now!

CARL (*Looks about him*) Right now? (*Decision*) OK, c'mon,
let's go —

They slip away and MARGARET *turns on her heel
suddenly aware of their absence.*

MARGARET (*Calling off, anxiously*) Frieda!

The DOCTOR *and* THOMAS *come forward to her,*
THOMAS *with the dress.*

DOCTOR You're absolutely sure this is the same dress that
you were wearing? I mean when that accident
happened?

THOMAS I'm sure. And I was there.

MARGARET Just stay out of it — would you!

THOMAS What? What?

MARGARET (*Now an angry yell*) Frieda!

THOMAS (*Here we go again!*) Oh, my lord! (*To* DOCTOR) Well?
What you want me to do with it? (*The dress*)

DOCTOR The one thing we must make sure is that he
doesn't catch sight of it. Until the right moment,
that is.

MARGARET Can't see what an old dress is going to achieve. It's
twenty years ago, for heavensakes — Where is that
girl?

THOMAS (*Surveying the place*) Quite a setup, ain't it? I mean,
the throne and all —

DOCTOR   It's all — specific. That's the nature of his madness.
          Specifics. This dress is specific. We will shock him
          in a very specific way.

THOMAS   Don't like the sound of that, I must say.

MARGARET My God, you're insufferable, you are!

THOMAS   What have I done now? He's simply nuts, isn't he?

MARGARET (*To* DOCTOR) You want proof? The dress? There!
          (*Photographs*) The pictures I told you about.
          (*Pointing*) There I am. (*Distressed*) Beside him. And
          there's the dress. Before he — fell — (*Breaks, whirls
          away again, calling*) Frieda!

DOCTOR   It is the specific details of his condition that are so
          extraordinary, lived out in such detail — see here —

> The DOCTOR *points at a detail in a photograph but
> the other two ignore him.* THOMAS *drapes the dress
> across the throne and stands, watching what follows
> between* MARGARET *and* FRIEDA. *The* DOCTOR *is
> poring over the photographs. When* MARGARET *calls
> again* FRIEDA *returns without* CARL.

FRIEDA   For God's sake, Mother!

> To her surprise MARGARET *grabs her firmly by the
> arm and takes her aside.*

MARGARET (*Fiercely*) You must stay away from that boy!

FRIEDA   Who? Carl — ?

MARGARET — away from him!

FRIEDA   C'mon! I'm nineteen years of age, for heavensakes
          — what's the big deal?

MARGARET You'll learn!

FRIEDA   Learn what?

> The DOCTOR *comes back to* MARGARET *and* FRIEDA
> with the photographs and THOMAS *joins them.*

DOCTOR   (*Pointing*) And who is this here? At the back?

THOMAS   I told you. That's me!

MARGARET   (*Looking at photograph*) Oh, my God, Frieda, darling! Look at that!

FRIEDA   (*Still angry with her*) What?

MARGARET   The likeness!

FRIEDA   You mean your old photo?

MARGARET   Not me! You! Don't you see? The living spit of you, exactly as you are now!

FRIEDA   Oh, Gawd!

MARGARET   — you tell her, Thomas — It's just like her, isn't it?

THOMAS   I'm staying out of this.

MARGARET   You would!

DOCTOR   I see the resemblance! Very interesting, yes mother, daughter —

MARGARET   Thank you, doctor.

THOMAS   Don't do it, doc, you'll only get burned.

MARGARET   God, you're a pain!

FRIEDA   (*About* THOMAS) He's always the same!

DOCTOR   But what's so wrong? A daughter looking like her mother?

THOMAS   You've just blown it, baby. All hell will break loose now —

MARGARET   Damn you! I know what you're getting at — my age, right? That's it, isn't it — more small-minded mockery —

DOCTOR   It's perfectly natural, mother, daughter —

MARGARET   — of course it is, perfectly natural, it's just that some people —

THOMAS   — it's just that I know —

MARGARET   — know what?

THOMAS   — what happens when you get on this kind of jag. OK? Who looks like whom, this picture, that picture. (*Hands up*) Whoom!

FRIEDA   Just stop it! Both of you!

MARGARET   That's right — stop it — it's my photo and I was just shocked to see Frieda there, not me —

THOMAS   But Frieda didn't see herself there, did you, Frieda? Frieda saw her Mum. As a young woman. Right, Frieda?

MARGARET   Sure! That's exactly my point! She can't see herself in me when I was her age. But I can. I mean, see myself in her as she is now —

DOCTOR Precisely. That's the mystery, don't you see —

MARGARET But Mr Know-all here misses the point, as per usual —

THOMAS Spare me!

CARL *comes back.* FRIEDA *is about to go to him again but is stopped by a glare from her mother.*

CARL You all set, doctor? Will I get him in here now? Henry?

DOCTOR What — who? Oh. No, not yet! Something else has just come up — the resemblance, you see, images that may trigger effects —

THOMAS Yes, professor; no, professor —

CARL Thomas! Do you mind? We're here on serious business —

FRIEDA Just ignore him, Carl!

THOMAS (*To Frieda*) Thought I was entertaining you, darling —

FRIEDA Entertaining, my foot!

MARGARET My mistake. Should never have brought him here in the first place.

THOMAS You simply can't do without me. My dear —

MARGARET Oh, no? Think again, buddy!

CARL Really, that's enough! The doctor has been invited here to carry out one of his trauma experiments. Isn't that right, doctor?

DOCTOR Indeed. Let me clarify something first. Why now? Why did you choose to call me at this precise time?

MARGARET (*Toward* CARL) It was his mother, I mean she was the one who suggested that we all come here. That was before she — she —

CARL My mother has died —

DOCTOR (*To* CARL) Oh, I am sorry. And she was Henry's sister, isn't that so? Your mother?

CARL That's right. Poor Mother! Well, before she died — just weeks ago, now — she told us that she believed

Henry might be, well, nearly cured.

DOCTOR Nearly cured. I see. Why? And why did she think that?

CARL That's it. She didn't say. All she said was that he was different now. Different. And that was when I saw about your shock treatment on the Medical Channel.

DOCTOR Hmm. (*Spells it out*) Essential Event Trauma Therapy. Actually. EETT, as a matter of record. So she came here, did she? (CARL *nods*) Your mother? And something he said, or did, maybe, led her to believe that —

CARL She said she felt it would take very little. To restore him. Her very words.

DOCTOR Very little, eh? Let me see that photograph again —

MARGARET For heavensakes, doctor, that old thing means nothing! I was just astonished at seeing Frieda in me, that's all.

DOCTOR Just allow me to use whatever I can. You see what I do is rather like a — reconstruction, a replay of some crucial incident. What you must understand is that, for him, reality is intolerable because it does not match what is in his mind. We have to encourage him to see that reality is tolerable, unthreatening. Even — dare I say it! — loving — (*To* MARGARET) That's why I wanted you to wear that dress. One more time —

MARGARET (*Very distressed, to* DOCTOR) Have you any idea what you're asking me to do?

DOCTOR Yes. I think so.

MARGARET *turns aside in distress.*

FRIEDA You OK, Mom?

MARGARET Should never have come here — thought it would help — him — can't go through with it — can't —

FRIEDA Carl! Look what you've done!

CARL What did I do?

MARGARET No — I'll be OK. The truth is always — so —

difficult —

THOMAS (*To* DOCTOR, *suddenly fretful, anxious*) And I suppose you're going to recreate that cavalcade? With us all on horseback again. That what you meant? Re-enactment of — what'd ya call it? — important events —

DOCTOR (*Remembering*) But, of course, you were there, too — when all this happened?

THOMAS Oh, I was there sure enough — dressed as Charles, Duke of Anjou. Looked terrific, if I say so myself —

FRIEDA (*Aside*) What a jerk!

DOCTOR And this cavalcade on horses? Was that Henry's idea?

THOMAS No. Mine.

MARGARET What? That's rubbish.

THOMAS Oh, no, it's not!

CARL For God's sake, don't start again! Doctor! Surely it doesn't matter a damn whose idea it was. It happened. He fell.

THOMAS But it *was* my idea! At first we thought of it as a movie. But then I thought — why not make it a real event — to be recorded on film, of course, but beyond acting, attempting to live it as it actually was. I had never seen Henry so — what's the word? — enchanted with the idea! (*Sense of power*) I watched his excitement. It was like a fever. He pored over the books I gave to him. Ravenous! Illustrations, pointing out this or that detail. He filled each of his houses with experts from the studios for months at a time, on costume, armour, the works — my idea — very definitely — yes —

DOCTOR But why did he pick on Henry IV?

MARGARET Because of me!

THOMAS Give us a break! It just happened to be his own name. Henry. He said: I will be playing myself! See? Joke! OK, forget it!

MARGARET No, it was because of me! I said I wanted to be Marchesa Matilda of Tuscany. I just picked the name out of one of his books. Just like that! I didn't even know who the hell she was. Then he told me. She was the woman who owned the castle at Canossa, the woman in the window with the old Pope while Henry kneeled in the snow outside. I will kneel at your feet. That's what he said to me. To the end of time. The two of us dressed up as deadly enemies.

DOCTOR Canossa — ?

CARL Yeah. Canossa. That's the scene they do here every day. The actors. Henry has to have this scene every damn day. I told you about it, remember?

DOCTOR But why this scene?

THOMAS Cop on, doc. (*Pointing to* MARGARET) Because she's in it! He's back there, twenty years ago! (*Sudden viciousness*) He's still on horseback and she's still screwing him —

FRIEDA Don't you dare speak of my mother like that!

MARGARET (*Troubled*) I was — very young —

FRIEDA You were nearly my age, Mamma!

MARGARET I wasn't as mature as you are, love. All I saw was this man with this absolute — adoration in his eyes —

THOMAS Which convinced you that he was an ass —

MARGARET You see, doctor, I was utterly spoiled, spoiled by attention, loved by him! — I found it — yes, he's (*Thomas*) right — found it ridiculous, absurd, but also, at the same time — with him — I think I was frightened, frightened by this intensity — terrifying. All the others laughed — this king stuff. I laughed, too. But I was really — afraid.

DOCTOR Afraid? I see. Excitable. Would you say he was the excitable type?

THOMAS And how! Sure. Excitable. But not normal. He was an actor, remember.

DOCTOR I beg your pardon?

THOMAS Sure, the oddest things excited him, but then you always knew that he was watching himself all the time.

DOCTOR Watching himself?

THOMAS Yeah. Acting. Cold, like. Observing himself all worked up. Yeah. Then he used to burst out into those strange attacks on himself, cursing himself, banging his head on the nearest wall.

MARGARET That's true. I'd forgotten about that. He used call himself the most dreadful names.

THOMAS He was some actor, actually —

CARL And since that accident he's become a terrifying actor, terrifying.

> MARGARET *turns sharply to* THOMAS *and his response, when it comes, shocks everyone into a moment's absolute silence.*

MARGARET (*Sharply, to* THOMAS) You hate him, don't you!

THOMAS (*Loud yell*) I made him a star! I made him what he was!

DOCTOR (*Breaking the shocked silence, eventually*) Hmm. I'd like to see a report of his actual injury. Later on, maybe.

> MARGARET *and* THOMAS *now go into a rapid, slightly dazed, double act. Very rapid exchanges.*

MARGARET — never forget it. Him lying there under the feet of the horse —

THOMAS — no one thought he was that badly injured —

MARGARET — funny thing — no blood or anything —

THOMAS — they just carried him upstairs —

MARGARET — then a couple of hours later —

THOMAS — in he walked —

MARGARET — the others — fooling about —

THOMAS — still playing our parts, see —

MARGARET (*Awakening from the double act*) Then it sank in, doctor. He wasn't playing a part. He wasn't wearing a disguise anymore.

THOMAS (*Still a bit dazed*) — there was a bit of horseplay, pushing and shoving, that kind of thing when, suddenly, he pulled a sword —

MARGARET He was the real Henry IV! No make-believe! It was unbelievable. He'd have killed somebody but that they jumped on him.

DOCTOR I see. Well. I've heard enough. The man was clearly disturbed even before the accident, in the grip of an obsession. The accident only froze it in place. You could think of it as a kind of — obstruction, blockage —

THOMAS (*Toward* CARL *and* FRIEDA, *pulling himself together with fake joviality*) Think of it, chickadees! You weren't even born then. And you (*Frieda*), you've now taken your mother's place in that photograph. What a bizarre place this world is when you think about it! The strange things that happen in time, a daughter becomes her mother while I go bald, and meantime he — Henry in there — is stuck in time, twenty years ago, nearly a thousand years ago — what's the difference?

FRIEDA You're a pain in the ass!

CARL Can we get on with what we have to do!

MARGARET (*Upset, to* DOCTOR) I can't wear that dress again, simply can't.

DOCTOR Well, actually, I now think your daughter might wear it instead!

FRIEDA What! Me!

Suddenly BERTOLD *comes running on, still in his courtier costume.*

BERTOLD That's it! I've had it! I'm out of here —

FRIEDA (*Screech*) Oh, Mamma, it's the madman!

MARGARET Who? Where?

CARL That's not him! Calm down, would you!

DOCTOR Who is this fellow?

THOMAS Another performer!

CARL Just one of the actors — (*To* BERTOLD) What the hell are you doing in here?

BERTOLD Like I said. Can't stand it any longer —

MARGARET Has he become violent? Henry?

FRIEDA Mamma!

MARGARET I must know!

BERTOLD No, ma'am, it's not the old man. It's those other three. They're the real nutcases —

LANDOLF *and* HAROLD *rush on in their costumes.*

LANDOLF There he is, the little devil. Got you!

HAROLD (*To* CARL) Sorry about this, sir. We'll take care of it. (*To* BERTOLD) OK, you! Back to work.

CARL What happened?

LANDOLF Oh, he made Henry blow his top, didn't you, you little rascal, you! Arrest him, Henry shouted! I will put him on trial! Take him to the throne room — wants to come in here and try him — what on earth are we going to do?

CARL Lock that door so that he can't come in!

FRIEDA Mom! I'm really scared!

HAROLD But Ordulf is in there with him. Alone. He'll never manage him on his own!

BERTOLD Sorry, sorry, didn't mean to cause all this — Sorry, forget it —

LANDOLF Just a sec! I've got an idea. Let you lot dress up as someone and we'll present you to him. Really! That'll calm him down. Always does, the costumes —

CARL Is that OK, doctor? Might be a good way for you to observe him?

FRIEDA I want to go home. Carl, right now!

DOCTOR He's not — armed — is he?

CARL (*To* FRIEDA) Just do this. For me. OK?

LANDOLF We've persuaded him never to carry a sword. We've had our scary moments with him (*Shrugs*) but —

FRIEDA I never wanted to come here. I only came because Mamma insisted —

MARGARET (*Almost to herself*) I want to see him — I must see him!

CARL The important thing is for the doctor to have the

chance to examine him.

DOCTOR (*Nervously*) You mean on my own?

MARGARET (*Loudly*) I insist on being there, too!

THOMAS But just a moment ago you said — Oh, I give up!

LANDOLF (*To* DOCTOR) It's OK. You'll all be in costume, playing roles —

THOMAS Costumes? You mean we gotta dress up? What is this?

LANDOLF Absolutely! If he sees you as you are he'll think *you're* in costume, and he'll fly into a rage —

DOCTOR Paranoid delusions —

MARGARET I can't wear that dress, not that!

DOCTOR (*Agitated*) Certainly not, this is not the time for that.

LANDOLF This'll be just a quick fix — to calm him down.

MARGARET If we must, we must. But what shall I wear?

THOMAS I don't believe this!

LANDOLF Perhaps Madame might play the part of his mother-in-law?

MARGARET Mother-in-law! Me? His mother-in-law?

LANDOLF In his fantasy he's married to Bertha. Her mother, his mother-in-law, that is, is the Grand Duchess Adelaide. You could be she. Don't worry, Grand Duchess Adelaide comes here often —

MARGARET You mean to say women come here to him?

LANDOLF Well, that happens to be his preference, ducky.

THOMAS *smirks at this and* MARGARET *turns on him in a fury.*

MARGARET And what the hell are you laughing at?

THOMAS Nothing! Nothing!

LANDOLF Bertold, take the Duchess off for robing!

DOCTOR And hide this dress, would you, somewhere out of sight, thank you —

FRIEDA (*To* CARL) Do *we* have to do this?

CARL No, come on, we'll wait outside —

BERTOLD (*To no one in particular*) I still don't get it, y'know —

BERTOLD, *carrying the dress, leads* MARGARET, CARL *and* FRIEDA *off stage.*

LANDOLF And you, doc, you get to be the Abbot of Cluny —

DOCTOR Abbot? Well, I suppose so —

THOMAS What about me? If she's staying, I'm staying.

LANDOLF Okeydokey — let me see — yeeees! You can be a simple friar, but holy of course. (*To* HAROLD, *off*) Harold! Do fetch the gear for these two, there's a dear —

DOCTOR He's not going to suspect me, is he?

LANDOLF Not in the least. Actually, the poor man, he's much more interested in the costumes than what's inside them. Fortunately. Besides, the Abbot and the Duchess are pals of his. They're the ones who got the Pope off his back in the end.

> HAROLD *comes back on with costumes. He and* LAN-DOLF *help the* DOCTOR *and* THOMAS *in robing.*

THOMAS You mean to say you've got all this stuff out there?

HAROLD Full costume department —

LANDOLF Each item designed to match his latest whim —

HAROLD When he asks for someone, that someone has to appear. Right away.

> LANDOLF *claps his hands, the stage-manager in action.*

LANDOLF Places, everybody! Let's go! Let's go! (*Calling off*) Madame! All powdered up out there, are we? Thank you! Harold, you go and help Ordulf prepare Henry for what's coming. OK?

> HAROLD *unlocks the door and exits.* MARGARET *makes quite an entrance as the Grand Duchess Adelaide to applause from the others.*

My, oh my! How divine! I must say I just love the

tiara —

MARGARET (*A fit of laughter, toward* THOMAS) Just look at you!

THOMAS I'm not any worse than the doctor there —

DOCTOR Normally I don't play parts myself in my sessions but this time, well —

A blare of trumpets, off.

LANDOLF That's it, everybody, that's the cue!

> *Door opens and* HENRY, *crowned, appears in full imperial regalia but over this he wears a rough sackcloth that trails in the dust.* HAROLD, *carrying sceptre and orb, and* ORDULF *walk behind him. Following the cue of* LANDOLF, *all bow low before this apparition.* HENRY *turns to the throne, removes his crown, and places it gently on the seat. Then he comes up close to examine his visitors.*

HENRY (*Royal dignity*) Your Grace — My Lord Abbot —

> *He sees* THOMAS *as the friar, jumps in fright, and rushes to* LANDOLF, *pointing.*

Who's that? Is that — Peter Damiani?

LANDOLF No-no, Your Majesty, this is just a simple monk accompanying the Abbot from Cluny —

HENRY No, it's not, it's that scoundrel Damiani, and (*To* THOMAS, *who is skulking*) stop trying to hide behind the Duchess, you, or I'll — (*Sudden switch to* MARGARET) Your daughter, I must speak to you about your daughter —

MARGARET (*Frightened, thinking of Frieda*) My daughter!

LANDOLF (*Heavy prompt*) The Empress Bertha, Your Grace, your daughter married to His Majesty, that is —

HENRY Shut up! The Duchess knows perfectly well who I'm talking about — don't you, madame?

MARGARET (*Uncertainly*) Ye-es —

HENRY Do you believe me when I say this? I've changed

toward your daughter — (*Sudden, violent shift, roaring toward the terrified* THOMAS) He's the one! Damiani! He stopped me from making the most terrible error of my life. Said he came from the Pope and that, under no circumstances, must I divorce my wife. Your dear daughter, madame. (*Sudden quiet*) How can I thank you enough, Peter Damiani? Otherwise I would have cast her aside — (*Sudden rage*) The bishops!

LANDOLF (*Warning*) Your Majes-tee!

HENRY I know — I know — I know — I mustn't speak of the bishops, no bishops, keep away from the bishops, bishops — my life, my whole life has been a total disaster — just look at me! All of you! Surrounded by corrupt, mendacious bishops! My mother, consider my poor mother, and now, here I am, a penitent in the snow before that lighted window, freezing — But that's enough of that. All that matters is — clarity, clear thought, lucid expression, yes, absolutely. Otherwise we do not — communicate — (*Another rush toward* THOMAS, *grabbing his monk's robe*) I kneel before you, Peter Damiani, and ask your forgiveness, forgive me, absolution, I beg of you — (*Kneeling, head bowed, the others looking at one another in consternation,* THOMAS *petrified. Then* HENRY *slowly raises his head, a wicked look at* THOMAS) Provided, provided, Peter Damiani, that you are not the one who — (*Wags finger*)

THOMAS Me? No, no — not me!

HENRY — started that rumour!

THOMAS Rumour. What rumour?

HENRY (*Roar*) That my beloved and saintly mother went to bed with the Bishop of Augsburg!

THOMAS No way — no way — not me — (*Appeal*) Somebody, please!

HENRY (*Peering into his face, dismissive*) No — not you — you wouldn't be up to it! (*Shift to the* DOCTOR) It's always others who are to blame, isn't it, my Lord

                Abbot? It's always them, them, them —

HAROLD   (*Prompts the* DOCTOR) Those rapacious bishops —

DOCTOR   Oh, yes, those rapacious bishops —

HENRY   Bishops? Bishops? Did I mention bishops? Who mentioned bishops? (*Up close to* DOCTOR) Did I ever tell you that I was but a little boy, six, when they took me away, said I was king. Can you imagine the effect of that, a child, a childhood destroyed, by privilege, power, immeasurable wealth, locked up, away from his mother, while they plotted and robbed —

LANDOLF   (*Softly*) Your Majesty —

HENRY   Right! No bishops! Leave out bishops. But this foul libel of my mother! That's something else again. (*Shift, up close to* MARGARET) You're a mother. You have a daughter. You'll understand. I cannot weep for my mother anymore. Why not? Can you tell me? Where are my tears? Mother — Just a month ago. She came here. From her convent. To see me. And now they tell me she is dead, but what I want to know is this: If you're here and I'm in sackcloth in the snow at Canossa, that means I'm now only twenty-six years old, isn't that so?

HAROLD   (*Gently*) In that case, Your Majesty, your mother is still alive —

ORDULF   (*Trying to help*) Yeah. Over in her convent, there, still going strong, she is, life and soul —

HENRY   True, true. Thank you. That's very helpful. I'm not in mourning now, no more mourning. (*Shift to* MARGARET, *flirty*) What do you think of my hair? Hmm? Nice dye job, no? Did it just for you when I heard you were coming. Let me see — but, of course, you've dyed your own hair since — Ho-ho-ho! Women, o-ho, women! I'm not shocked. Why should I be? We are all desperate to fight the future while it rushes toward us, faster, faster — Maybe the Abbot could answer — yes, in matters of birth and death try the clergy. What do you think, my Lord Abbot? Did you ask to be born? I certainly didn't. Did any of us? So, what's going on here? What's it all about, eh? Answer me! No answers — Deadly treadmill, day after day, on, on, unable to do anything about it, something bigger than all of us, something out there, among the stars — maybe — controlling — the great machine —

DOCTOR   (*Not quite knowing what to say*) True, too true —

HENRY   (*Whirls away from the* DOCTOR) But! Big but — once we give in, and most of us do, oh yes, the daily — routine, the endless boredom, each day the same as the last, and what happens? We *desire*! Our secret desires fester inside us, to be what we are not! So! We perform! Performance! This woman wants to be a man, that man wants to be a woman, this old man wants to be young again, oh Christ, the pity of it all. Then out comes the paintbrush, the whitewash, the dye, the role-playing, the images thrown upon the blank surface! (*Grabs the* DOCTOR *again*) Look at you! Look at your holy robe, the sleeve, the sleeve, see what's slithering away down there, like a snake escaping, you can't do a thing about it, there it goes, off, life slithering away — I can't look at my face in the mirror anymore. Disgusting! (*Turns, grabs* MARGARET *violently so that she screeches*) Why did you do that to me, why? Why?

LANDOLF   (*Trying to stop him*) Your Majesty — time to rest!

HENRY   Do you look in the mirror? Of course you do, constantly! (*Now turning on* THOMAS) And you, Peter Damiani, how could you take up with that gangster, no, I won't say his name but I — (*To* LANDOLF *and* HAROLD *who are now holding him*) It's alright. I'm finished. Can't make a point anymore without — But I will! For example, it's perfectly clear to all and sundry that we hold on tight to the image that we have of ourselves. True or false? No answer. What does it matter who dyes his or her hair? No one is fooled. It's just that we have this image of ourselves and in the sad fashion of human beings we dye our hair. Why? Just to fool that image in the mirror. For a few minutes, perhaps, until (*Slowly*) we — have recovered — ourselves — (*To* MARGARET) You remember, madame, remember your beautiful blonde hair? Or was it auburn? Or black? Can't remember — You know what the difference is between us? You dye your hair for real, but I know it's only an image, a fading image — (*Turn, rage*) And you, Peter Damiani, trying to conceal what you were back then! Won't work. Not with me, damn you! (*Tearing at the sackcloth*) And this — this — off, off —

ORDULF You poor man, take it easy, now —

HAROLD Sire! You must remain penitent in the presence of the Pope —

HENRY (*Waving the sackcloth about*) Never! I, Henry, King of Germany and Holy Roman Emperor, do declare that tomorrow, at Brixen, twenty-seven imperial bishops will sign my deposition of Pope Gregory VII —

LANDOLF Oh dear — now-now, Your Majesty — !

HAROLD Sire, you cannot say such things!

LANDOLF There now — there now — Look! The Duchess and the Abbot and this gentleman have come to help you. (*Cue*) Isn't that so, Madame, Monsignor, help you, come to —

DOCTOR Oh, yes-yes, come to help —

LANDOLF (*Directing the* DOCTOR) — intercede with the Pope —

DOCTOR Oh yes. Indeed. Exactly! Intercede with the Pope —

HENRY (*Throwing himself on his knees, to* LANDOLF *and* HAROLD) Sackcloth! Cover me with sackcloth! At once! (*They drape him with the sackcloth*) Forgive me, Lord Abbot, and you, Madame, forgiveness! Forgiveness! Absolution! Cleansed! Thank you, thank you!

> *He prostrates himself fully before them while they look at one another: What next? Moment's silence. Then* HENRY *rises slowly, looks at them, then grabs*

LANDOLF *and pulls him aside.*

HENRY (*Pointing at* THOMAS) One thing I can't do is —
grovel — before that — that — creature there!

LANDOLF Who?

HENRY Damiani!

LANDOLF Now-now! We've told you, Your Majesty, thou-
sands of times, that's not Peter Damiani. No way.

HENRY (*Confused, frightened*) It's not? Are you sure?

HAROLD My liege, he's only a poor monk —

HENRY (*Whirling about and grabbing a scared* MARGARET)
You'll understand! You're a woman, it's our instincts, you see, when we give in to our instincts,
there's no knowing what — It's true, by the way, I
mean about your daughter, I've changed toward
her and now love her. (*Whirling about on* THOMAS)
And don't you say otherwise, damn you! (*Groans,
trying to curb himself, takes* MARGARET *aside, now
almost conversational*) She's here, you know, your
daughter!

MARGARET What? How do you know that?

LANDOLF (*Warning*) Madame!

HENRY (*To* LANDOLF) Shut up! (*To* MARGARET) Your daugh-
ter — out there — but maybe you know already?
Hm? Do you? Know already? Hmmm? Out there?
Daughter?

MARGARET (*Almost fainting*) Please —

LANDOLF (*Cue* MARGARET) Lady Bertha, that is —

HENRY Silence! (*Back to* MARGARET) She's out there. In the
snow, with me, following me, out of love, frozen,
two nights in the open before that window, the
two figures looking out at us, that woman and the
Pope — You must — you must, with the Abbot
here, you must ask, petition, plead with the Pope
on my behalf — Promise!

MARGARET (*Near collapse*) Promise —

DOCTOR Yes-yes, of course we'll ask — Pope —

HENRY (*Shift, manic joke*) He's a magician, you know, our
Pope, magic man, can make things disappear —

Whut! Gone! He can raise the dead. 'S true. What I really want him to do is free me from what I was! Have you any idea, have you any notion of what it is like? Any of you? To be imprisoned, forever, in a twentysix-year-old body? Do you know what it's like? Hmm? No answers. (*To* MARGARET) I want to love your daughter — as she should be loved — That's it! That's all! I have finished. Thank you! Dismiss! Madame! (*Bows*) Lord Abbot! (*Bows*)

> *He sweeps away quickly,* LANDOLF, HAROLD *and* ORDULF *following him.* THOMAS *turns aside toward the throne, at which point* HENRY *turns smartly again, rushes to the throne, picks up the crown and puts it under the sackcloth. He leers at a shaken* THOMAS *and sweeps away again with his three attendants.* MARGARET *collapses into a chair.*

THOMAS That's it! Let's get out of here!

DOCTOR (*Rapidly*) That woman — his sister — she was right! It will take very little to bring him to — You see, my original idea was to have her put on that dress, twenty years ago — the shock of that — but then I thought the young girl — the image as it was for him, I mean as she (*Margaret*) was twenty years ago — she said it herself, like her daughter. But now I'm thinking — Canossa — the snow, the lighted window —

THOMAS Wouldn't matter a damn who puts on what dress — the guy's completely loco —

DOCTOR You think so?

THOMAS Should be in a proper hospital. Instead of these damned games —

DOCTOR Games. Precisely. That's the best way of understanding this. Games. Deadly games. You see, he knows perfectly well that we are disguised, playing our roles —

THOMAS You mean to say that he knew who we were! Christ!

DOCTOR — as a child knows and goes along with it, but for him it was real whereas he knows we were pretending but he has to keep up the pretence. Otherwise, he would have to face the intolerable and walk out that door, into the street and back into real life — intolerable —

MARGARET (*Scream*) He recognized me!

> *The other two are shocked at this. As the* DOCTOR *speaks another panel slides open high above, perhaps larger than any before, and* HENRY *steps into view, observing, listening, a dark Prospero.*

DOCTOR Yes. Yes, that's what we were saying just now. He became suspicious. All madmen are suspicious. Because they are desperate to preserve the image of themselves which may indeed be a multiple of images, each contending, the image in the mirror, the sly attempts at make-up —

MARGARET No! No! You don't understand! He knew me as I am!

THOMAS Oh, come off it! The guy's nuts!

MARGARET I could see it in his eyes! Not madness. Recognition, a reaching out —

THOMAS But he was talking of your daughter, what's-her-name? That Empress dame —

MARGARET (*Rush*) — then when he talked about my dyed hair. 'You remember your beautiful auburn hair?' he said, and it was true, doctor, my hair was auburn, just like my daughter's — and that's why he was talking so much about her —

THOMAS For God's sake, he doesn't know your daughter, never even met her!

MARGARET Of course! You know nothing about anything, you! He meant me, as I was then, isn't that right, doctor, when he said my daughter he meant me?

THOMAS She's nuts! I'm nuts! We're all nuts!

MARGARET You! You're a reprehensible, uncaring, monstrous person, you —

THOMAS   Look! You were his mistress, once upon a time.
          Fact. You were never his wife! In the real world or
          the unreal world. Neither. But in this mad world
          of his just now you were this Duchess dame, OK?
          — whose daughter was this Empress chick that
          married him. Simple? No? Or am I missing some-
          thing?

MARGARET Of course he has never actually met Frieda. No
          one says he has. How could he tell what colour her
          hair is?

THOMAS   He was generalizing, that's all, about hair and stuff.

MARGARET He was talking about me! Me!

THOMAS   Look at the way he behaved toward me!

          *The DOCTOR, who has been half listening up to this,
          is now fully alert.*

MARGARET (*With a force that surprises even herself*) You know
          damn well why he was so hostile to you!

          *Long pause: MARGARET and THOMAS have a
          momentary stand-off. She is thinking of how he
          replaced Henry. He is thinking of spiking the horse
          in the cavalcade and causing Henry's fall. Then they
          both think of their present unhappiness together.*

DOCTOR   Well! I shouldn't make too much of it, really. He
          was introduced to the Duchess and the Abbot and
          of course he became suspicious of a third, un-
          named person — suspicion, always suspicion —

THOMAS   See! Peter What's-his-name —

MARGARET Doctor! Do you think it's possible? That he actually
          knew who I was?

DOCTOR   Maybe. Actually, I was going to say there was
          something in his manner which was — and I hate
          to use this word — normal. There is a common
          rigidity in the insane, a fixity as if everything were
          frozen — not him. Even his mood swings had a
          certain — looseness to them — as if the role he was

playing offered him — relief. That is why I consider him a very suitable candidate for my EETT treatment. It works particularly well, you know, with actors. I had thought to dress you (*Margaret*) in that dress of all those years ago. Then I thought — your daughter. You said she looked like you, back then —

MARGARET She must be kept out of this!

DOCTOR Even if she is the one who brings him back?

THOMAS But you were the one who brought her here — why did you bring her here, then, if you didn't want her involved?

DOCTOR Canossa! They perform that scene every day for him. Very well. Let's perform it for him now. The woman. The Pope. In the window.

MARGARET I will have nothing to do with this!

DOCTOR No — your daughter will play this woman — in the window —

MARGARET — my daughter!

DOCTOR Exactly! In that dress! Why, I myself am happy to play the Pope! D'you know, I think I'm rather getting to like this acting —

THOMAS Madness! Madness!

MARGARET (*Screams*) Frieda!

> *Above them,* HENRY *raises his arms. A flash of dazzling light and a blare of trumpets. Upstage, a nervous* BERTOLD *appears out of the darkness.*

BERTOLD (*Announcement*) Ladies and Gentlemen! Her Grace, Her Excellency, Her — the Marchesa of Tuscany!

> *Behind him appears* FRIEDA, *a delicate beauty in her mother's old, flowing dress. The figures of the young men and* CARL *behind her and to one side, but in the shadows. The* DOCTOR *and* THOMAS *freeze in place, their backs to this scene. But* MARGARET *sees it, then turns aside with an anguished cry.*

MARGARET Frieda!
   FRIEDA (*Calling tentatively*) Mother?

> *The lights come down to a single bright spot on her.*
> *Quick blackout.*

ACT TWO

Music. Wind and snowstorm.

HENRY alone centre stage in his penitential garb, struggling in a windy snowstorm before a tower. The throne has been removed. On the screens a shadowy film crew with camera, lights, etc, facing out to audience as if filming HENRY. These images of the film crew fade and give way to snow falling as HENRY battles his way toward the foot of the tower. A lighted window in the tower and in it the haughty, remote figures of FRIEDA as the Marchesa of Tuscany and the DOCTOR as Pope Gregory VII.

Unlike the earlier Canossa scene, this one is played for real. HENRY prostrates himself before the figures in the window three times and then sinks, crouched, as the figures in the window disappear and the snowstorm ends. HENRY rocks on his heels, well upstage, groaning and gathering his penitential robes about him, his back to audience.

Downstage, the DOCTOR, still wearing part of his Pope costume, carefully leads on MARGARET, wearing her contemporary clothes, and FRIEDA, costumed as the Marchesa. Behind them come CARL and THOMAS in their contemporary clothes. They all take in the slumped figure of HENRY.

MARGARET Are you quite sure about this?

DOCTOR Absolutely.

FRIEDA Can I get out of this damned dress?

DOCTOR No-no, not quite yet — we're not finished —

FRIEDA Well, can we just do it now? I'm bursting inside this dress. Mamma, what size were you? — Can't believe it —

MARGARET Oh, darling, I was just a waif then — a waif —

FRIEDA Tell me about it!

MARGARET (*Of* HENRY, *to* DOCTOR) You sure he's OK back there?

THOMAS OK? Him? You gotta be kidding.

CARL (*To* THOMAS) Please! Now what, doctor? (*To* HENRY) Will I get him down here now for the next — ?

DOCTOR (*To* CARL) You know your mother was absolutely right —

CARL My mother?

DOCTOR Yes. It's going to take very little more — one final shock — to bring him fully back to his old self again —

MARGARET (*Fervently*) Oh, I want that! I want that to happen!

THOMAS Oh. You want that, do you? (*Heavy irony*) Great! Terrific! Smashing! She wants him back!

MARGARET Get lost!

FRIEDA I don't want to go through any more of this! Carl!

CARL You just gotta be here. That's all. Right, doc? That's all she's gotta do? Be here?

FRIEDA And what if he attacks us?

DOCTOR Attacks? Good heavens, no!

CARL We'll all be outside that door over there — There's no danger —

DOCTOR Look! He's absolutely calm now, almost as if he were — sedated —

FRIEDA — and all we gotta do is — approach him? That it?

DOCTOR — show yourselves to him —

FRIEDA Show ourselves? And do what?

DOCTOR Nothing. What he'll see is you (*To* MARGARET) as you are now and then you (*To* MARGARET) as you were then (*To* FRIEDA) on that fateful day of the accident —

MARGARET And that's going to bring him back? Looking at both of us like that?

DOCTOR I've no doubt whatsoever — everything else has prepared him for this moment.

THOMAS Let's see — you really want that guy to jump from this (*Margaret*) to this (*Frieda*)? Or maybe it's the other way round? Ya know what that's gonna do to him? He'll go ape! Twenty years? More like nearly a thousand years! It's gonna cream him, doc. You're gonna be sweeping him up off the damned floor with a shovel —

MARGARET   You're so crude!
THOMAS   Crude? Oh, yeah, sure! Maybe I'm the only one round here who faces up to what's what —
CARL   Can't we just go ahead and, like, do it!
FRIEDA   This is real creepy!
THOMAS   That's right! The only one who actually calls it like it is —
DOCTOR   Sir, you're clearly incapable of seeing what is happening here. Yes, that's right! A single, shocking step across a void. Remember the old play? An old blind man is persuaded to step off a cliff, when in fact he is standing on a level floor. The human mind will accept anything, my friend. Provided there is a key to unlock it!
MARGARET   (*Loudly*) I want some time alone — with Frieda.
FRIEDA   Oh, Gawd! What is it now?
MARGARET   — alone — (*To the others*) If you don't mind?
DOCTOR   Very well. Call out if you need us —

> *He gestures to the others. He and* CARL *leave but* THOMAS *lags behind.*

MARGARET   And what do you want?
THOMAS   I think I should stay.
MARGARET   You're the one person who shouldn't even be here.
THOMAS   You know you're trying to humiliate me!
MARGARET   Not difficult —
FRIEDA   I'm leaving —
MARGARET   Oh, no, you're not! (*Pointing*) He is!
THOMAS   I don't get it. You've completely changed towards him, haven't you? Remember? Back then? You used to say he was monstrous towards you. So? What's the deal? You gonna give me some daylight?
MARGARET   Yes. Most of my life — I think I've been living with — lies. Lie after lie —

> THOMAS *pauses, then leaves quickly.* MARGARET *and* FRIEDA *draw close together downstage during*

the following.

FRIEDA You OK, Mom? (*No response from* MARGARET) Don't know what the hell I'm doing here either — this creepy place, wearing this ridiculous dress, like some weirdo, alone with — that — that crazy back up there! (HENRY, *still prostrate*)

MARGARET (*Very disturbed*) He's not — He's your father!

FRIEDA (*Shocked pause*) What? Just say that again — slowly.

MARGARET (*Deeply distressed*) I said — Yes! Your father —

FRIEDA Come on! My dad's dead — that's what you always said, right? Died before I was born — you said —

MARGARET What else could I say?

FRIEDA Hold it right there! You mean you lied to me —

MARGARET — Yes! No!

FRIEDA — all those years! (*Looking back at* HENRY) That thing! Jeez — don't believe it!

MARGARET (*Hysterical*) Wasn't lying! Least not in the beginning — for me he was — I mean, dead — the same thing — incurable, that's what they told me — he will never come out of that place again! Ever! That's what they said —

FRIEDA (*Trying to make sense of it*) It's just come back to me now, the way you used to hate me watching those old movies of his — had no idea. Turn that thing off, you used to holler. Couldn't figure it out — always wondered why your reaction was so — so extreme —

Images of Henry's movies flash on the screen as the two women are lost in memories. HENRY *rises behind them, turns toward them, and begins to come up slowly behind them, without their seeing him.*

You know — all this — it had better be a bad joke —

MARGARET No joke — until today — I didn't know but now I

think I know — I think I can face the truth —

FRIEDA (*Bitterly*) Ya know, I mean, like, I used to wonder which of your male buddies might qualify as my daddy —

MARGARET Don't, Frieda —

FRIEDA Will I pick this one or that one? This guy would make a nice daddy. No? (*Savagely*) Who else knows this?

MARGARET No one. (*She tries to reach out*) Frieda —

FRIEDA (*Screams*) Don't you dare touch me!

> *The women move apart from one another and as they do they become aware of* HENRY *right up behind them.*

HENRY (*From one to the other*) Which role shall I play, hmm? (*To* MARGARET) For you? (*To* FRIEDA) Or you? I can play anything, you know. Change my face. Throw off the years with a flick of the wrist. Good, evil, no problem. (*Pointing to stomach*) It's all in here. In the gut. Yep! The whole human comedy. Male, female, or in between. King or clown. They say I'm a — chameleon. Do you know what that's like? To be able to change? To have an endless appetite to perform? Your mind races with the energy of what is possible. You feel you can do anything! And then, when you give yourself to the role, all that energy pours out and sometimes you are left with — nothing!

MARGARET Oh, my God, he *is* better! He is!

HENRY Better? Better-better-better? Better than what? (*To* MARGARET) Shall I play to you? (*To* FRIEDA) Or to you? Hmm? Wrinkles or smooth flesh? The autumn of life. Or its precious spring? What-is-now? What-was-then? You see, that's the mystery of acting. You can defeat the body. For a few moments under the lights you have this illusion of immortality. That great surge of power that you feel is your mockery of death. (*Yell*) Turn on the lights! Let the performance commence!

>FRIEDA *watches what follows with open-mouthed amazement.*

MARGARET   (*Cry*) Henry! Please —

HENRY   (*Antic, ignoring her*) Yes? Did someone call? Who called? Yes?

MARGARET   Don't be like that! It's me! Margaret!

HENRY   Recognize that voice? No, definitely not! — Who-who-who?

MARGARET   Stop it! Stop it!

HENRY   Stop it? What is this *it* that has to be stopped? Hah?

MARGARET   I want you, Henry —

HENRY   Want-want-want?

MARGARET   I want you as you were —

HENRY   As I was!

MARGARET   — as you were — back then —

HENRY   Back then? But back then I would not want you — as you are now! No? True or false?

MARGARET   Please, Henry, don't! Please —

HENRY   (*Roar*) No, back then, I wouldn't want you as you are now — Yes! — I would want you as you were — *You!*

>HENRY *whirls on a terrified* FRIEDA *and grabs her. Before she knows it he is assaulting her, kissing her, trying to tear her clothes off. She yells and* MARGARET *screams, launching herself at* HENRY.

MARGARET   Monster! Monster! She's your daughter!

>HENRY *stops, shocked.* FRIEDA *staggers to one side trying to recover.* HENRY *looks sadly at her and raises one hand toward her in shocked recognition, an appeal, at the same time knowing that all is lost. At once, the* DOCTOR, CARL, THOMAS, LANDOLF, ORDULF *and* BERTOLD *come rushing on and encircle*

HENRY *and the two women. All watch as* HENRY *makes that futile hand gesture toward* FRIEDA.

FRIEDA (*To one side, in deep shock, almost to herself*) I gotta get out of this — ridiculous — dress.

All watch as she staggers off, slowly. MARGARET *rushes after her.*

MARGARET (*Scream*) Frieda! Frieda!

CARL, THOMAS *and the* DOCTOR *hurry off after* MARGARET.

DOCTOR (*As he goes, to the young men*) You guys take care of this!

The four young men look at one another and at HENRY *who stands, lost, to one side.*

BERTOLD OK, what do we do now?
LANDOLF (*Gently, to* HENRY) Your Majesty?
HENRY Majesty-majesty? That what you said? Well, if I am a king — where is my throne?
LANDOLF (*To* HAROLD *and* ORDULF) Bring on the throne!
HENRY No! Stop! No throne. That's finished!

He grabs a startled BERTOLD *and takes him, intimately, to one side.*

'Have you a daughter?'
BERTOLD Whatja mean a daughter? Whatja getting at? Hey! Let me go!
HENRY 'Have you a daughter?'
BERTOLD Oh, yeah! I get it now! (*Acting as Polonius*) 'I have, my lord.'
HENRY (*Distraught*) 'Let her not walk i' th' sun. Conception is a blessing, but as your daughter may conceive, friend, look to 't.'

BERTOLD (*To the three others*) See! That's all the old guy wants
— just wants to act, play Hamlet, get it?

HENRY Act? Act? But, of course, you're right, my friend.
We're all in a farce. Have been, for years. Didn't
you see them? Those out there? The fools, all
dolled up in their outfits, mouthing their lines. I
did that, you know. I was the one who put them
through their paces, the ringmaster, blithering
idiots, thinking they're one thing when they're
really something else. And that bitch! Duchess,
indeed! Ha-ha-ha-ha-ha! Oh, my lord! What a
sight! That charlatan doctor spouting his clichés!
And him! Him! That gangster along with them,
Peter Damiani, my ass! I'll get that guy, if it's the
last thing I do. Did you see the fear in their faces?
Hmm? Terrified that they would be revealed as
they really are. Little did they know that I saw
through them, naked! Pitiful, empty, costumes,
masks, faces — the whole fol-de-rol — (*All four
young men*) What are you staring at? Damn you!

BERTOLD What's he doin' now? Is he acting again?

LANDOLF What's he saying?

HAROLD What's happened?

ORDULF He seems OK!

HENRY *watches them for a moment, then he roughly
pushes them apart. He pursues them, driving them
with his words while they stagger about, stunned.*

HENRY That's it! All over! Done! Finished! You hear?
Game's up! I've had enough of it — By God, what
a nerve she has, her coming here like that, pretending, putting on a show of concern — even — yes
— love, after all those years, safe, thought she was
safe, did she? Feeling safe before this — this —
lunatic! Flaunting herself like that! And him!
Bringing him with her, just like that, after all that
he did, the bastard! Well, this time they're not
getting away with it, by God, no, no way. Thinking

that they can parade me around, putting me through the hoops, he'll do this, do that, locked into this deadly routine, monkey in his cage, that's what they want, is it? Well, they're sure in for one hell of a shock. Looking forward to just seeing their faces, plus that idiot doctor, oh, yes, especially him. Labels. That's how it works, you know, how the whole ramshackle farce of a world is kept spinning. Stick labels on poor fools. Keep them in their places, this one's mad, that one's sane. And people play the roles that are given to them, course they do. See! Click, click, everyone in place, don't step out of line, now! Do you think I was any different when I fell off the horse and banged my head? Course not. I am what I am what I was. Why are you looking at one another like that? I get it! You're thinking: Is he or isn't he? Ha-ha-ha! (*Roar*) Of course I'm mad! Of course I'm Henry IV! On your knees, assholes! Kneel! Down! Bend! Kiss the ground! (*Forcing them to kneel*) Or, by God, I'll — ! Up! Get up, damn you! Bloody sheep! Power, that's what power is. Know what it is? Nothing. Just words, performance, show! *Puff!* Gone on the wind! But people are fooled, people want to be fooled. I tell you, I've learned so much. Learned what an amount of — pretence, sham, is needed to oil the wheels. Just to keep the powers that be in place, this idiot in his palace, that idiot on his presidential lawn. What a charade it all is! What theatre! And my daughter. They brought my daughter with them.

HAROLD   Your daughter? Who's your daughter?

LANDOLF   Frieda! Is Frieda your daughter? Oh, my God!

HENRY   I can never confess to anyone what I have done —

ORDOLF   You can tell me, my liege.

HENRY   Liege! No — not that. Just — talk to me.

BERTOLD   Hey! Is he acting again?

HENRY   You! What's your name?

BERTOLD   Me? They call me Bertold.

HENRY No, damn you! Your real name!

BERTOLD Joe.

HENRY You look like a Joe. (*To* LANDOLF) And you?

LANDOLF Bobby.

HENRY Bobby. Suits you, too. (*To* HAROLD) And you're — ?

HAROLD Nick.

ORDULF (HENRY *looks at him*) Jock.

LANDOLF Oh-my-heavens, this must mean that you're completely — my, how wonderful!

HENRY You sure about that? Wonderful? I've listened to you, you know. From out there. In the night. Talking among yourselves. Using your own names. Normality! Hah! Well, then. Let's have normality! Let's have a good laugh. Let's laugh at those idiots out there who still think I'm mad. Ha-ha! Laugh, damn you, laugh! No laughs? You look terrified, the four of you. Are you afraid I'm slipping back into that pit again?

> *On the screens, whirling images of bedlam, white shrouded figures on the corridors of a mental hospital with Henry's tortured face imposed upon them all through the following speech, then blank.*

Have you ever wondered why people are so terrified of the mad? Hmm? Because of that awful difference that they see? No, not at all. It's because of the similarities that they notice, same bodies, same looks, same smiles, but then! The threshold can be so easily crossed — (*To* HAROLD) Look me in the eye! Yes, you're still terrified —

ORDULF I'm not.

HENRY No, no, you're not. You're different to the others — You — belong in here —

LANDOLF You mean? — all this time! — you've been — pretending — mad — king —

HENRY You've got it in one, sweetheart!

HAROLD But for how long?

HENRY Years!

HAROLD Jesus!

> BERTOLD *tries to slip off but* HENRY *spots him and stops him in his tracks.*

HENRY Hey! Where d'you think you're going? Joe!

LANDOLF But, heavens! We don't even know what to call you now.

HENRY Henry! Call me Henry. Hello, Henry! How ya doin', Henry! There! Simple, no? Do you know what I really think of those three out there? One is a whore, another is a quack, and the third is a homicidal prick. You think I exaggerate? And who'd believe me if I said that? He's mad again, the poor dope. Listen to his wild talk! (*Break, sudden overwhelming grief*) My daughter! I have lost my daughter! (*Almost immediate recovery*) Actually, the amount of stuff we observe every day which appears mad is quite extraordinary. But we don't stop and dwell on it. If we did we'd rapidly go round the twist. Know what I mean? Course you do. (*To* BERTOLD) Can you see into what I really am? No, of course you can't. No one can see into another person. Ever. We kid ourselves that we can, but no way. We say I know that person as well as I know myself. Rubbish. All we're left with is whatever that person chooses to offer us. But at this stage in human history that's a banal idea, isn't it? What is more interesting is how people get by on the surface, nowadays everywhere surfaces, surfaces, screens, flickering images, no depth — that is why we must constantly invent — love — (*Grabs* LANDOLF) Do you think she will forgive me?

LANDOLF (*On cue*) Of course — my liege. Of course she will forgive you. You mean the Marchesa, don't you? (*Gestures to the others for help*) We are all your loyal servants here, aren't we, gentlemen!

BERTOLD That the dame in the window, right? Margaret? The one on horseback, right?

HAROLD   Sure — yeah — we all think you're a great star, don't we, guys?

BERTOLD   Ya wanna we play some other parts? We could maybe make a small movie — or something —

HENRY   Stop! You fool! (*To* LANDOLF) I mean my daughter! I have been playing the penitent — in the snow — for years. It was like being in the half-light. I never knew why I was seeking forgiveness. It was my role, you see. But now my role has ended and I see my sin for what it is. My daughter! My daughter! I never knew her, all those lost years, never knew she even existed. (*Walks about, very disturbed*) It has suddenly gotten very dark in here, hasn't it?

ORDULF   You want your lamp?

HENRY   Ah, Ordulf, isn't it? Ordulf with my nightly lamp.

ORDULF   Ya want it?

HENRY   Don't you know that as soon as I go out with my lamp at night you guys turn on all the lights in here and have a ball.

LANDOLF   Shall we turn on all the lights then?

HENRY   No — that would be too much — not quite ready for such — clarity — yet! (*To* BERTOLD *and* HAROLD) fetch me my throne, would you? — And you, Ordulf, my lamp — and my book —

> BERTOLD *and* HAROLD *go off.* ORDULF *lights the lamp and brings it to him.* HENRY *takes it and* ORDULF *goes and fetches a large vellum book and quill.* HAROLD *returns, pushing the throne.*

Hey! Where is that other one? Our friend, Joe?

HAROLD   He just disappeared out there! Turned my back, he was gone, *vamoose!*

HENRY   Don't like that. Not to be trusted, our friend Joe.

LANDOLF   (*Calling*) Bertold! You-eeee —

HENRY   Never mind. Forget him. (*Sits on the throne*) Here! Come and sit around me, come on, one last time, as we've done over the years, sitting, relaxed. (*The three sit, a bit self-consciously*) Relax, for heavensakes! Relax. Pity there's no moonlight effect. Atmosphere. King with loyal courtiers. Nice picture, no?

LANDOLF My God, if we had known this all along —

HENRY What? What would you have done? Hmm? I'm interested.

LANDOLF We could have known we were only acting, I mean —

HAROLD We thought ourselves into thinking it was for real —

HENRY Real? Of course it was for real —

LANDOLF But you've just told us —

HENRY Just give yourselves to it! Nearly a thousand years ago in the court of King Henry IV where everything is unchangeable, nothing can be altered and one is free of the monstrous uncertainty of the here and now! Don't you see its appeal? Event follows event as laid down in the book, the freedom of it, the relief, the absence of — choice. Too bad, it's all over. (*Gets up and breaks the group*) I've had it. By Christ, I'll be revenged on her and her clown of a doctor, not to mention that cur that she's taken up with — he's the one! Just wait!

ORDULF Your book — I brought your book —

HENRY — book?

ORDULF — to record your words for today —

HENRY All that I have now, Ordulf, all that is left to me is contained there, in that book, in your hands —

ORDULF (*With quill*) Will you dictate, Your Majesty?

HENRY Yes-yes-yes. Let me see — I do believe we had reached the Peace of Mainz, if I remember correctly, and its effects upon the common people. But tonight — tonight I want to record something else. Something personal. How we deal with our innermost illusions, our worst fears, our failures, everything that we have lost, our secret histories —

The DOCTOR *and* THOMAS *come on and stand, observing the scene of* HENRY *and the young men at the throne.* HENRY, *alone, ignores this intrusion, as if the two weren't there.*

THOMAS Quite some scene, no? Maybe we should go get the cameras?

DOCTOR So! We've been pretending, have we?

THOMAS OK, break it up, you guys! We've had enough of this.

DOCTOR No, just a moment. This isn't unusual, you know, when the patient enters the twilight zone between madness and a return to sanity, pretence, faking it, often happens, rather like struggling against the full exposure to the light again.

THOMAS You guys in on this scam?

LANDOLF I beg your pardon!

THOMAS Been having us on, right, just for the dough?

LANDOLF I would have you know, sir — we are professionals!

HAROLD How did you get to know? Who told you?

THOMAS That other little jerk — that actor — told us out there — everything — said this was all just a set-up, years of it — can't believe we were all taken in like that —

HENRY (*Great roar*) Judas!

For a moment HENRY *seems about to attack* THOMAS, *then* CARL *rushes on and straight up to* HENRY.

CARL All that time! You were pretending — and my mother? Pretending to her, too? Your own sister, how could you, uncle?

HENRY Go on! Keep going!

CARL As she was dying — your own dead sister!

HENRY It's not only your sister's going to die — I promise you —

CARL Not my sister! Your sister, damn you! You made her play the role of your mother, Agnes, even as she herself was dying —

HENRY Your mother!

CARL   Of course.

HENRY   (*Yell*) Agnes was the mother of Henry IV and therefore I have spent years weeping for her. (*Frantic*) Where is the Marchesa?

THOMAS   Don't let him do this! Don't you all see? He's up to his old tricks again!

HENRY   (*Turning on him*) Tricks? Who said tricks? (*To* DOCTOR) You're a medical man, right? (DOCTOR *nods*) You were the one who got these to dress up, play these parts. (*Yell*) What right have you to play with my deepest feelings like this? Because I was mad? That it? Do you realize you could have made me mad again? After all those years —

DOCTOR   How many years, by the way? How many years have you been pretending like this?

HENRY   (*Casually*) Four, five —

THOMAS   Five years — now *that's* crazy, man! Real crazy!

HENRY   (*Calls off*) Margaret! She has to be here before I can go on and — (*Quick turn on* THOMAS) Remembered nothing — that horse — that fall — But you! I remember you! (*Back to* DOCTOR) Actually, doc, it's a great case history. You should write it up. Man locked into mad fantasy, then, one day, he awakes, slowly, like finding the use of your limbs after a long paralysis, eyes opening as if for the very first time. Birth again. Of course, the first thing I thought — Throw open the windows! Run out and tell everyone! Then I saw what was outside there and I said — no — (*Rush to* THOMAS *again*) Look at my hair — look at my hair, damn you!

THOMAS   Well, I've gone grey too —

HENRY   Different. I did not know that I was aging — until it was too late. (*Roar*) Who pricked the horse behind me and caused my fall?

Long pause. HENRY *doesn't look at anyone and waits. The others all shuffle about, uncomfortably.*

CARL   What? What do you mean, the horse? What

happened?

HENRY (*To* DOCTOR) Yes, my dear doctor, very interesting case history — it's wealth, you see, you begin to believe that you can buy everything, I do believe that that was my true insanity, the insanity of power — whereas, of course, everything is beyond our control and sooner or later we will all hit our heads on the ground —

BERTOLD *comes on quickly. Again,* HENRY *is the only one who doesn't react to him.*

BERTOLD She's gone, folks — taken off — that young chick, Frieda — just like that — into the four-wheeler and *varooom!*

MARGARET *slowly follows him on, carrying the dress that* FRIEDA *had been wearing. Again,* HENRY *doesn't look at her, but everyone else watches her with attention. She walks up to* HENRY *and lays the dress at his feet.*

MARGARET It's what you wanted, isn't it?

HENRY *picks up the dress and looks at it, closely.*

HENRY (*To no one in particular*) It's clothes, you see. The trouble all started when the ape first tried to cover himself —

THOMAS Let's get the hell outta here —

DOCTOR No! Be quiet! Let him speak!

HENRY (*With dress*) Cover her body — 'Cover her face, mine eyes dazzle' —

MARGARET (*Scream*) You've destroyed her!

HENRY Margaret —

MARGARET Years of self-indulgence! Make-believe! Not able to walk out and face reality. Look at me! See what twenty years has done. Look at me, damn you!

HENRY Now that you're here everything can come out

into the open — at last —

MARGARET The open! Don't make me laugh! Twenty years!

HENRY (*Roar*) Yes, twenty years! You — you and that scumbag there (*Thomas*) — you condemned me — to perform endlessly — to play that role — without end —

> *The screens light up: The cavalcade of costumed figures on horseback as in the beginning of the play, Henry and Margaret as Henry IV and Marchesa of Tuscany.*

(*To* MARGARET) What role were *you* playing? Hmm? Back then? All those years ago?

MARGARET What're you talking about?

HENRY Marchesa, indeed!

MARGARET What a fool I've been! Hoping against hope! Believing in something that didn't exist.

HENRY Or slut? Hmm? Were you playing the slut? With him! (*Thomas*)

> *On the screen the image of Henry thrown from his horse.*

THOMAS (*Grabs* MARGARET) C'mon — let's go —

HENRY Who pricked the horse and made me fall?

> *As* THOMAS *and* MARGARET *begin to move away* HENRY *moves with great speed, pulls a dagger from* LANDOLF's *belt, and stabs* THOMAS. MARGARET *screams.* LANDOLF, HAROLD *and* ORDULF *drag* HENRY *away while* BERTOLD, CARL *and the* DOCTOR *help* THOMAS.

CARL Good God! He's knifed him!

DOCTOR Get him (*Thomas*) out of here! Quickly!

> *A weeping* MARGARET *and the* DOCTOR *help* CARL *and* BERTOLD, *lifting, dragging a gasping* THOMAS

off. HENRY *and the other three young men stand frozen in place.* HENRY, *watched closely by the three young men, goes wearily and sits upon the throne.*

HENRY Come and sit with me!

The three exchange looks and then take their old places about the throne, LANDOLF *and* HAROLD *extremely apprehensive,* ORDULF *indifferent.* BERTOLD *comes on in a state.*

Ah, it's you! Come! Join us!

BERTOLD (*Shaking his head*) You wasted that guy! He's dead!

He staggers off again.

HENRY (*To the very uncertain group around him*) Pay no heed to him. Let us just — be together as we've been in the past. Shall I tell you why I couldn't leave here? Hmm? When I came to my senses — what an odd phrase that is! — I looked out there — and you know what I saw? Extinction. I saw the species moving toward extinction. Waste, mountains of waste. Everything — used up. No fuel, no water, no food. A cold darkness descending. And I said to myself, yes, yes, it is better in here.

LANDOLF and HAROLD look at one another. HENRY and ORDULF are both impassive. On the screens images of desolation and destruction. Above these the floating image of the dress worn by Frieda and the young Margaret, an image of colour flying in the air.
Lights down.